$30. -

Bloom's

GUIDES

Mark Twain's
The Adventures of Tom Sawyer

The Adventures of Huckleberry Finn
The Adventures of Tom Sawyer
All Quiet on the Western Front
Animal Farm
The Autobiography of Malcolm X
The Awakening
The Bell Jar
Beloved
Beowulf
Black Boy
The Bluest Eye
Brave New World
The Canterbury Tales
Catch-22
The Catcher in the Rye
The Chosen
A Christmas Carol
The Crucible
Cry, the Beloved Country
Death of a Salesman
Fahrenheit 451
A Farewell to Arms
Frankenstein
The Glass Menagerie
The Grapes of Wrath
Great Expectations
The Great Gatsby
The Handmaid's Tale
Heart of Darkness
The Hobbit
The House on Mango Street
I Know Why the Caged Bird Sings

The Iliad
Invisible Man
Jane Eyre
The Joy Luck Club
The Kite Runner
Lord of the Flies
Macbeth
Maggie: A Girl of the Streets
The Metamorphosis
Native Son
Night
1984
The Odyssey
Oedipus Rex
Of Mice and Men
One Hundred Years of Solitude
Pride and Prejudice
Ragtime
A Raisin in the Sun
The Red Badge of Courage
The Road
Romeo and Juliet
The Scarlet Letter
A Separate Peace
Slaughterhouse-Five
The Stranger
A Streetcar Named Desire
The Sun Also Rises
A Tale of Two Cities
Their Eyes Were Watching God
To Kill a Mockingbird
Uncle Tom's Cabin
The Waste Land
Wuthering Heights

Bloom's

GUIDES

Mark Twain's
The Adventures of Tom Sawyer

Edited & with an Introduction
by Harold Bloom

BLOOM'S
LITERARY CRITICISM
An Infobase Learning Company

Bloom's Guides: The Adventures of Tom Sawyer
Copyright © 2011 by Infobase Learning
Introduction © 2011 by Harold Bloom

Bloom's Literary Criticism
An imprint of Infobase Learning
132 West 31st Street
New York NY 10001

Library of Congress Cataloging-in-Publication Data
Mark Twain's The adventures of Tom Sawyer / edited and with an introduction by Harold Bloom.
   p. cm. — (Bloom's guides)
   Includes bibliographical references and index.
   ISBN 978-1-61753-000-5 (hardcover : alk. paper) 1. Twain, Mark, 1835–1910. Adventures of Tom Sawyer. 2. Adventure stories, American—History and criticism. 3. Sawyer, Tom (Fictitious character) 4. Boys in literature. 5. Mississippi River—In literature. 6. Race relations in literature. I. Bloom, Harold.
   PS1306.M38 2011
   813'.4—dc22
                                        2011000966

Contributing editor: Portia Williams Weiskel
Cover designed by Takeshi Takahashi
Composition by IBT Global, Troy NY
Cover printed by Yurchak Printing, Landisville Pa.
Book printed and bound by Yurchak Printing, Landisville Pa.
Date printed: June 2011
Printed in the United States of America
10 9 8 7 6 5 4 3 2 1

This book is printed on acid-free paper.

Contents

Introduction 7

Biographical Sketch 9

The Story Behind the Story 15

List of Characters 21

Summary and Analysis 24

Critical Views 61

   Henry Nash Smith on Tom Sawyer, Inadequate Hero 61

   James M. Cox on Play, Pleasure, and Showing Off
      in the Novel 65

   Judith Fetterley on Tom as a
      Local Antidote to Boredom 70

   Lee Clark Mitchell on Appearance
      and Voice in the Novel 75

   E.L. Doctorow on the Child Reader
      and the Adult Reader 78

   Albert E. Stone Offers Some General Remarks 81

   Michael J. Kiskis Reconsiders Twain's Values 86

   John Bird Examines Twain's Double Narrator Strategy 91

   Harold K. Bush, Jr. on Attitudes Toward
      Religion and the Village Church 98

   Roy Blount, Jr. on Twain as Political Commentator 100

Works by Mark Twain 105

Annotated Bibliography 106

Contributors 113

Acknowledgments 116

Index 118

Introduction

HAROLD BLOOM

At 80, rereading *Tom Sawyer* is an adventure in nostalgia. Unlike Twain's magnificent *Huckleberry Finn*, it is essentially a boy's book but with a saving difference. James Cox, an old friend I recall with affection, thought Sawyer's tale a tribute to the force of play. The great heroes and heroines of play are Shakespeare's Falstaff and his Rosalind and the two giant forms of Cervantes, the Knight of the Sad Countenance and his squire, Sancho Panza. That is too formidable a literary company for Tom Sawyer to join, but Cox nevertheless tracks Twain's perspective on his entertaining protagonist.

Huck is more than an entertainer, unlike Tom, yet *Huckleberry Finn* is one of a handful or so of essential American classics, with *Moby-Dick*, *The Scarlet Letter*, *Leaves of Grass*, Emerson's essays and journals, Emily Dickinson's poems, and one or two more. There is little that is profound in Sawyer's adventures though much to be enjoyed.

Admirably controlled, the implicit ironies of the book are easy to overlook and constitute a persistent hum or undersong throughout. Decidedly not a Christian, Twain avoids a satiric tone while presenting the conventional pieties of church, community, and conduct. Respectability, into which Tom must grow and which Huck always will refuse, constitutes a demarcation the story is not allowed to transgress. Twain was fond of saying that the United States was a Christian country and so was Hell.

In any work of authentic literature, everything has the status of metaphor unless a game is being portrayed. When Tom plays, his adventures can take on the aura of realistic representation and his book rises into a limited splendor. Falling back from play, we are given household and school, and our interest declines.

Why then does *The Adventures of Tom Sawyer* retain permanent value? Partly we sense that Twain is learning his craft, measuring his energies and perceptions while he seeks an adequate image for his storytelling desires. Though Huck is present in Tom's story, he is there as a potential icon of Twain's narrative invention. When Huck begins to speak for himself in the later book, Twain's genius emerges abundantly and with amazing joy. Tom Sawyer is an antechamber to that American triumph, which it foretells but does not share.

Biographical Sketch

According to Roy Morris Jr., author of *Lighting out for the Territory: How Samuel Clemens Headed West and Became Mark Twain* (2010), the writer we know as Mark Twain gave himself some other names as well. "Sam" and "Sammy" are unsurprising; "Youth"—his wife's name for him—perhaps emerged from a funny episode. The monikers he considered for his nom de plume before deciding on "Mark Twain"—"Thomas Jefferson Snodgrass," "W. Epaninondas Adrastrus Blab," "Grumbler," and "A Dog-Be-Deviled Citizen"—are intriguingly bizarre. Australian critic Clive James observed that Twain was "democratic all the way down to his metabolism" ("The Voice of America," *The New Yorker*, June 14, 1993, 81), and author-humorist Roy Blount Jr. calls Twain "America's Original Superstar" and suggests that his satiric wit animates the likes of Jon Stewart and Stephen Colbert (*Mark Twain Anthology* 467).

Mark Twain is the fictional persona of Samuel Langhorne Clemens, born 1835 in Florida, Missouri, the next-to-last of six children in the family of John Marshall Clemens, who was descended from pioneer, slaveholding farmers, and Jane Lampton, who descended from Kentucky Indian fighters and slaveholders. Looking back on his life, the author recalled his improbable survival after birth: " . . . I was [said to be] a sickly and precarious and tiresome and uncertain child, and lived mainly on allopathic medicines during the first seven years of my life" (Paine, ed., *Mark Twain's Autobiography* vol. 1, 108). Twain went on to become one of the most robust, prolific, adventurous, and creative of American citizens.

The iconic southern town featured in *The Adventures of Tom Sawyer* (1876) and *The Adventures of Huckleberry Finn* (1885) was a fictionalized version of Hannibal, Missouri—where the family moved in 1839 and where Mark Twain staged his own rambunctious childhood. The following recollection is an early indication of something notable about the author—whether his imagination, youthful insecurity, or his gift for telling "stretchers." Twain describes being mistakenly left behind when the family set out:

Toward night, when they camped and counted up the children, one was missing. I was the one. I had been left behind. . . . I was well frightened, and I made all the noise I could, but no one was near and it did no good. I spent the afternoon in captivity and was not rescued until the gloaming had fallen and the place was alive with ghosts. (Kiskis, ed., *Mark Twain's Own Autobiography*, 112)

Scholars of Twain's life have ascertained that the accidentally left-behind son was not Twain but his older brother, Orion.

Mark Twain emphasized the use he could make of his own experiences—his "usable past"—for his writing. Recollected from the vantage point of 30 years, the author's childhood supplied abundant material for *The Adventures of Tom Sawyer*. "In Hannibal," Twain recalled, "the sun rose upon a tranquil world, and beamed down . . . like a benediction." Novelist and critic E.L. Doctorow reflects on Twain's imagining ". . . Hannibal renamed St. Petersburg in the book, [as a place where] a person needed no education, social position, money, or renown to feel the radiance of heaven. He didn't even need shoes" (*Anthology* 365). Many of the novel's playful pastimes and risk-filled adventures, along with the darker episodes marked with fearfulness and confusion, were largely Twain's own; his childhood was a mix of scholastic and domestic duties with plenty of free time for discovery and self-invented adventures. Adult life, by contrast, was full of tedium, ritual, duty, and hypocrisy—reason enough to inspire the town's most clever and perceptive resident to leave home when he was able to seek a much larger stage for his life's drama.

Twain's childhood unfolded in a slaveholding state and his lawyer/father sold slaves and prosecuted abolitionists. As children invariably do, Twain unconsciously absorbed the dominant racial attitudes of his time and place with no incentive to question their legitimacy. Later in life, with the mind-opening insights that came with travel, new acquaintances, and the liberating influence of his wife's family, Twain took up issues of imperialism and social injustice and made conscious acts of atonement toward black people with all manner of benevolent gestures. At the end of his life he was perceived by many as a social reformer whose writing expressed a heartfelt democratic sensibility and came down on the side of justice for all.

John Clemens's death in 1847 compelled son Samuel to work at odd jobs to help compensate for the poverty his family now faced. His formal schooling ended about the same time, and by 1851 (at age 16), he began working for the Hannibal newspaper, purchased a year earlier by Orion. In 1853 he left Hannibal for St. Louis and the East Coast, where he worked as a journeyman printer and wrote short travel pieces and sketches for various newspapers. In 1855 he returned to St. Louis and began his brief (and well-paying) career as a riverboat pilot on the Mississippi. His training included familiarity with nautical language like *mark twain*, a term indicating a river depth of two fathoms and thus safe passage ahead.

Mark Twain did not become "Mark Twain" until he was 27 and a journalist in the Nevada Territory. Fred Kaplan, one of many Samuel Clemens biographers, points out the appropriateness of "twain," a word suggesting division of one into two, for a man in need of an alternate identity (*Singular* 1). Critic Forrest Robinson elaborates on this observation, pointing out that "Mark Twain" encompasses a multitude of personae:

> The Mark Twain of "The Celebrated Jumping Frog of Calaveras County" is an effete if rather myopic and humorless Eastern lawyer, who succumbs without knowing it to the wiles of garrulous Simon Wheeler. He is distantly related to the avuncular, mildly condescending Mark Twain who presides over *The Adventures of Tom Sawyer*, but altogether remote from the complexly "innocent" traveler in *Roughing It*. . . . The fictional Mark Twain is thus no singular thing but rather a varied cast of characters. (*Historical Guide* 14)

The dilemma—who should call him what?—gradually became natural to all. Kaplan writes, "The man and the pseudonym had grown comfortable with each other. In that sense, Clemens/ Twain increasingly became a single figure, even to himself" (1).

The outbreak of the Civil War in 1861 ended commercial steamship passage on the Mississippi leaving Mark Twain to join an ineffectual, quickly disbanded, and possibly apocryphal state militia. This turn of events left the headstrong and ambitious young man the chance to leave home and "head out for the Territory." Twain left that same year with Orion, who had been appointed governor of the Nevada Territory by Abraham Lincoln. The next years were predictably full of adventures: prospecting for silver and gold, meeting literary notables Artemus Ward and Bret Harte, writing a hoax about charitable funds raised for Union soldiers, fleeing to San Francisco to escape a duel, and visiting Hawaii. Critic Roy Morris Jr. suggests that readers would have been treated to more colorful and scurrilous adventures in *Roughing It*, Twain's account of those years, had he not felt the need to spare his refined and scrupulous young wife embarrassment (Morris 2).

Mark Twain's writing up to this point centered mainly on journalism, with some travel sketches appearing in publications in different parts of the country. Money did not come easily at first, and he supplemented his small journalist's pay with stipends for lectures given at various venues. The famous jumping frog story that Twain adapted and embellished from an old bartender's tale brought his first (and instant) fame as a writer when it was published in 1865 in the *Saturday Press*, a New York publication, as "The Celebrated Jumping Frog of Calaveras County." This early success set the stage for the launching of a major American writer with *The Innocents Abroad* (1869), *Roughing It* (1872), *The Gilded Age* (1873), *The Adventures of Tom Sawyer* (1876), and *The Adventures of Huckleberry Finn* (1885).

A singularly happy and sustaining feature of Mark Twain's life was his marriage to Olivia Louise Langdon. While living in San Francisco in 1866, the ever-restless Twain arranged with his editor at the time to participate in a tour of Europe, Egypt, and Palestine on the steamship *Quaker City*. Having acquired by then his persona of freethinking writer, he attracted the attention of Charles Langdon, the young son of a liberal religious family interested in abolition and social justice, who showed Twain a picture of his sister Olivia (Livy). Charles later invited Twain to New York City in 1867 to meet his family (including Livy) at a New Year's Eve public reading by Charles Dickens. From that evening to Thanksgiving 1868, Twain worked to win favor from not only Livy but her mother, who worried that her daughter's suitor was not quite substantial enough to marry into the family. The couple married on February 2, 1870, at the family's beloved summer home in Elmira, New York, where the family spent part of every summer. Twain's private study there looked over the hills and provided peaceful solitude for his writing. Twain remarked once to William Dean Howells: "After 30 days, I go to Elmira, 1,000,000 miles from New York" (quoted in *Cosmopolitan Twain* 233).

Twain had a good marriage and children he adored, but these blessings also brought personal tribulation and abiding sadness. His brother Henry's death in a steamboat accident (1858) was the first of the traumatic losses sustained during his lifetime. Twain's firstborn son, Langdon Clemens, died in 1872, not yet two years old. Daughter Susy was born that same year, and her own premature and sudden death in 1896 from spinal meningitis left Twain bitter and inconsolable. When his wife died in 1904, he described his heart as being "hurt beyond healing." He wrote: "I am a man without a country. Wherever Livy was, that was my country. And now she is gone" (*Singular* 614). That same year daughter Clara entered a sanitarium and daughter Jean began having seizures. When Jean died in 1909, only Clara remained. She married in the same year and gave birth to Mark Twain's only grandchild, a girl, whom he did not live to see and who committed suicide in 1964. No heirs remain.

In his final years, Mark Twain relied on good friends and his own strength to survive. Jean's death was another impactful loss, but he took some comfort knowing her suffering—lasting many years—was finally at an end. He wrote to Clara: "Of my fair fleet all my ships have gone down but you; but while I have you I am still rich" (quoted in *Singular* 653). This fragile gratitude was not enough to overcome the effects of his angina and increasing frailty and moroseness; his comments during these years sounded unmistakably nihilistic. In early 1910, sensing the nearness of his death, Twain cut short his visit in Bermuda to make an uneasy voyage back to his home outside Hartford, Connecticut, where he died peacefully with Clara and family friends in attendance. Alongside family members who had predeceased him, he was buried in the Elmira cemetery.

Mark Twain—his presence and influence—continues to show up in a variety of places, even gardening magazines. (An editor must have thought readers would focus better on the dangers of lightning if Mark Twain were in on the warning: "Thunder is good, thunder is impressive; but it is lightning that does the work" [*Organic Gardening*, June/July 2005, 64]). We speak of "the Gilded Age" in American history without knowing it was Twain who named it thus. President Franklin D. Roosevelt took the term *New Deal* from Twain's writings, and each year the Kennedy Center honors America's funniest people with the Mark Twain Prize.

Mark Twain looms as a romantic, larger-than-life figure. Biographer Fred Kaplan calls him "the Singular Mark Twain." A curious feature of the writer's life is the familiarity most people feel with him. Newspapers announced his death as if it were a personal loss. "How many of us feel . . . [that Mark Twain] wrote . . . for us, with the intimate frankness of a friend talking over a cigar?" asked the (NC) *Wilmington Morning Star* ("A Brief Biography," *Historical Guide* 13). An oft-made observation about Mark Twain's readers is that so many of them assume they have read more of the author's work than they actually have—probably because his work is woven so indelibly into American culture. He fused and transformed diverse subjects and styles of writing into a memorable achievement and wound his way through several careers. "I *have* had a call to literature, of a low order—i. e. humorous," he told his brother (*Mark Twain's Letters, Vol. 1*, p. 322), but his impact and influence during his lifetime were recognized with the awarding of three honorary degrees—by Yale University in 1901; by the University of Missouri in 1902; and by Oxford University in 1907. Mark Twain is also—perhaps most memorably and significantly for his country—emblematic of the human capacity to rise above the limitations and narrowing prejudices of one's personal history to arrive at a humane and generous, no matter how pessimistically humorous, view of the world.

14

The Story Behind the Story

When American essayist Ralph Waldo Emerson issued his famous challenge to all Americans to declare their cultural independence from "Old World" ways of writing and thinking (*The American Scholar*, 1837), he could hardly have imagined a more robust response than the one Mark Twain would be making 40 years later writing *The Adventures of Tom Sawyer*. The novel is a portrayal of community life in a small village along the iconic Mississippi River where the residents, old and young, established and marginal, poor and not so poor, go about the business of living, all of them flawed in some way, some egregiously. It is quintessentially an American story told in American speech. Twain's cleverly offhand depiction of the mainly harmless hypocrisy that permeates most of these social interactions adds to the appeal of the novel.

The distinctively American flavor is especially evident in Twain's use of what was becoming recognized as the characteristic American voice, the vernacular speech of ordinary citizens of the time. To underscore how informally foreign, if not "aberrant," that American speech seemed to Old World readers, it is useful (and entertaining) to read in an early English review praise for Twain's comic talent followed by a lament wondering "whether it would not have been as well if [the non-conversational parts of] the book had not been written more uniformly in [proper] English" (the *Athenaeum*, June 24, 1876, 851; reprinted in Hutchinson, *Mark Twain: Tom Sawyer and Huckleberry Finn*, 11–12). In the century since his death, it is Twain's replication of ordinary American speech that has made his novel both appealing and enduring. Students of Mark Twain will come upon many critical pieces praising the author's elevation of the vernacular to the level of art. (See especially Sieglinde Lemke, *The Vernacular Matters of American Literature* [2009] and the Ken Burns 2001 PBS documentary on Mark Twain.) Lemke quotes critic Lionel Trilling's words of praise for the way Mark Twain's writing established . . . the virtues of American colloquial speech . . . [which] has nothing to do with pronunciation or grammar. It has something to do with ease and freedom in the use of language. . . . with the structure of the sentence, which is simple, direct, and fluent, maintaining the rhythm of the word-groups of speech and the intonations of the speaking voice. (53–54; originally cited in Barry A. Marks, ed. *Mark Twain's "Huckleberry Finn,"* 1959, 51)

Lemke adds: "In writing a novel in the vernacular, in the common speech of 'ordinary' Americans, Twain made crucial headway in dismantling America's inferiority complex" (54). This assessment of Twain's achievement is widely shared by readers and critics alike and is the reason most often cited for the novel's historical and cultural significance.

Twain received plenty of criticism as well, specifically, in the case of *Tom Sawyer*, his first full-length novel, for what critic John Bird calls the author's "[narrative] weakness" (*Mark Twain and Metaphor* 55). Bird cites another critic, John Gerber, to describe what many have noticed about Twain's narrative style:

It is a shifting style because the point of view slides from that of a middle-aged writer to that of the approximately twelve-year-old boy. As the middle-aged author, Twain writes in the conventional, stilted, "literary" manner that characterizes other novels of the period. But when he adopts Tom's point of view, his language immediately freshens. The boy forces him to do what he does best: report concrete happenings in simple pictorial language. (55)

Other critics lament the vacillation Twain's readers must navigate without the help of satisfying transitions between colloquial conversation and formal narrative, between the main character's voice delighting in its own antics at center stage and the author's staid and condescending voice describing and simultaneously judging those same antics. Bird comes to a different conclusion, asserting that the author is deliberately creating both voices—the lively and irreverent Tom Sawyer and the unimaginative "grown-up" narrator, whose very conventionality undermines itself in favor of youthful fun and inventiveness. Bird writes, " . . . the conventional narrator . . . is not the familiar Mark Twain, but another persona, one that we are supposed to recognize and reject. There are *two* narrators here [and] the novel is richer for it. . . ." (59).

Critical assessments like these remind us that the apparent simplicity of *Tom Sawyer* can be deceptive. Differing perspectives and observations about Twain's methods and motives make for a more complex reading of the novel without detracting from its cheerful depiction of rambunctious and liberated youth. (For readers caught up with the adventures, dangers, romancing, and all the clever ways Tom and his companions outsmart adults, the novel remains fully entertaining.) Another critical and related problem is the ambivalence Twain is known to have felt about what audience he envisioned for his novel— whether it was to be a book of adventures for boy readers or a book about a boy's adventures for adult readers. This dilemma became the subject of a prolonged dialogue between the author and W.D. Howells, an established literary figure of the times, editor of the *Atlantic Monthly*, and personal friend. (Those interested in their correspondence will find a full account in the 2007 Norton Critical Edition of *The Adventures of Tom Sawyer*.) Twain was dissuaded from following his first impulse to create entertaining boyhood adventures for nostalgic adult readers and to continue Tom's life through adolescence into adulthood. Howells and his own wife argued that an exciting book of adventures for boys would also be eagerly read by adults. Twain himself had come to realize that Tom Sawyer might end up a pretty dull boy had he been allowed to reach adulthood.

With the publication of *Tom Sawyer*, Mark Twain not only earned fame for rescuing American literature from Old World conventions, but he was also credited with writing the novel that has come to be recognized as the best portrait of American boyhood. Some dissent over that view has emerged, however, and new students of Twain will discover recent commentary discussing whether the novel celebrates the spirited and inventive antics of the American boy's liberated imagination or whether it leads to the conclusion that these very qualities depend ultimately for their significance and pleasure on the restraining (and ultimately triumphant) influence of adult authority. Some dissent also comes from those who find Tom's actions and attitudes inconsistent with one particular year of boyhood. Tom seems adolescent in his innocent romancing of Becky but more like an eight-year-old when he digs for treasure or plays silly pranks on his elders.

Acquaintance with the literary subgenre known as boy culture allows for a richer and deeper understanding of Twain's novel. In the beginning of the mid-nineteenth century, little boys were permitted to leave the constraining influence of matriarchal authority and domesticity. They wore old trousers (the origin of "play clothes"?), roamed around in little gang-like bands, had adventures, played pranks, and were generally unruly, sometimes cruel and delinquent. Their antics generated widespread lamentations in the general community, but the consequence of this freedom for boys—learning the skills of courage, competition, and autonomy for adulthood—was too highly valued to bring this cultural practice to an end. In his novel, Twain also grappled with the righteous outrage and Sunday school sentimentality that were increasingly detectable in contemporary stories about boys both like and unlike Tom Sawyer. He wrote two entertaining parodies of these attitudes. "The Story of the Bad Little Boy Who Didn't Come to Grief" (1865) is about Jim who, among other things, stole jam from his poor mother's winter supply and hid his transgression by refilling the jar with tar without a twinge of conscience. "The Story of the Good Little Boy Who Did Not Prosper" (1870) is about "Jacob . . . [who] always obeyed his parents, no matter how absurd and unreasonable their demands were." When Jacob, however, sees Jim stealing apples from a tree and piously reads to him from a book about how bad boys stealing apples fall out of their trees and break their legs, Jacob suffers the broken leg when Jim falls out of the tree on top of the boy without breaking his own. (These stories are included in the Norton Critical Edition of *The Adventures of Mark Twain*, pp. 225–31.)

The first edition of *Tom Sawyer* was published (without illustrations) in England on June 9, 1876. On December 8, 1876, the first American edition (illustrated) was published by Elisha Bliss and his American Publishing Company of Hartford, Connecticut. Twain had outlined the plot of the novel in 1873, had begun his sustained work on it in 1874, and—after completing 500 pages—stopped abruptly, stating that "[his] tank had run dry" (quoted in Quirk, *Mark Twain and Human Nature*, p. 87). From other autobiographical sources and correspondence, Twain revealed that running out of material had not been the problem—he had plumbed his memory for details of his own boyhood and found plenty—but, rather, that his ambivalence about his audience and how old he should allow his young hero to become had stymied him. For almost a year he tended to other parts of his life before resuming work the following summer in 1875. Then one day in July, he wrote to Howells to triumphantly announce the novel's completion. Revisions and more editing followed, but his first novel was essentially ready for publication.

Early sales in the United States were disappointing despite Howell's praise-filled review following the English publication. English reviews were generally favorable although many (like the review previously cited) favored the undeniable humor over the vernacular speech. One anonymous reviewer was pleased to report that reading about Tom Sawyer sent a "youngster" into peals of laughter (*Critical Essays* 23). Another predicted that little English boys would find the "strange" American language ("although founded upon English, is yet not English," 35) highly entertaining. Most American reviewers were as measured in their assessments as the English but over different issues. One warned that it would be imprudent "to put the book into the hands of imitative youth" (62). Another lamented that "so fine a fellow as Tom lies and smokes" (63). Another looked beyond the main character to praise Twain's "humorous and acute delineation of the follies, superstitions and peculiarities of boys, girls, and older people" (59). (A collection of reviews for all of Mark Twain's publications can be found in *Mark Twain: The Contemporary Reviews*, ed. Louis J. Budd, Cambridge University Press, 1999.)

Over the years hundreds of editions of Tom Sawyer have been published, and it has been translated into more than three dozen languages. An edition appearing in 1936 contained illustrations by Norman Rockwell. At the time of Twain's death, Tom Sawyer was his bestselling novel. It is still widely read and appreciated, although its sequel, *The Adventures of Huckleberry Finn*, has attracted the most critical attention because the novel's racial themes are complex and controversial.

List of Characters

Tom Sawyer, literature's enduring and endearing rascal, exemplifies the high-spirited playfulness and adventurous abandon associated with a traditional and romanticized notion of American childhood. Whether a sentimental projection of Twain's own boyhood persona or an authentic embodiment of rebellion, Tom himself spends his time outsmarting adults and having fun with his mainly benign antics.

Aunt Polly is the guardian of Tom Sawyer and his half brother, Sid. She is alternately exasperated with Tom (who seems to be her favorite) and amused by his antics. She has the appearance of a devout southern woman but is not without her vanities and occasional misjudgments.

Huck Finn is the "outsider" who understands "insiders" better than they do themselves as he is independent of social identities and pretensions. Huck's dialogues with Tom provide much of the humor in the novel. Huck lives by pluck, luck, and superstition, and he often goes hungry.

Joe Harper, one of Tom's friends, is game for most, but not all, of Tom's schemes and adventures. With both parents still living and caring for him, Joe is almost a "normal" rascal.

Ben Rogers, a showoff, impersonates larger-than-life subjects to get attention. He is Tom's first "victim" in the whitewashing prank.

Willie Mufferson, an anemically "Model Boy" and "pride of all Mothers," appears only once in the novel, when he accompanies his mother to church. Understandably, the other boys despise him.

Alfred Temple, the "new boy," challenges Tom to a fight and loses. Becky uses him to make Tom jealous, and he, in retaliation, pours ink on Tom's spelling book.

Sid Sawyer, another rascal but not a likeable one, is Tom's little half brother; he feigns virtue when Aunt Polly is around but otherwise occupies himself with underhanded ways to get Tom in trouble.

Mary is Tom's kind and cooperative, if somewhat bland, cousin. She lives in Aunt Polly's household, but what she does and how old she is are not made clear.

Becky Thatcher, with her blond curls and sweet smile, is a timid and conventional presence in the novel who adds humor to the story when she plays Tom against her other "suitors" and drama when she gets lost in the cave with Tom. Twain equips her with traditional nineteenth-century feminine wiles, and she wins Tom's heart in an unblinking instant.

Amy Lawrence instantly loses her status as Tom's first girlfriend the moment Tom's eyes fall on Becky Thatcher, the new girl in town. Amy, despondent, is shifted to the background until she briefly reappears later as a foil in Tom's scheme to make Becky jealous.

Reverend Sprague has an exaggerated notion of his rhetorical skills, which, when fully called upon, put all members of his congregation to sleep. Tom's bug tricks easily upstage the reverend in church.

Judge Thatcher, Becky's father, appears in the Sunday school episode as "altogether the most august creation [the] children had ever looked upon." To protect others from getting lost, he seals the cave entrance, unwittingly causing the grisly death of Injun Joe.

Mister Dobbins, the thoroughly unlikable schoolmaster, is humorless and punitive. One of the adult "show-offs," he gets more pleasure from flogging students than from teaching them. For revenge, the students take advantage of his balding head and a feisty cat to play an embarrassing trick on him on the last day of school.

Injun Joe, the town's resident "half breed," is more of an outcast than Huck; because he is a "non-entity," townspeople unreflectively transfer all their fears, suspicions, and guilt onto him. He is deserving of his menacing reputation when Tom and Huck witness his murder of Doctor Robinson and subsequent framing of the innocent and hapless Muff Potter. Injun Joe remains a major character in Tom and Huck's adventures, providing elements of legitimate terror and dread to their otherwise mainly benign escapades. Critically, the Injun Joe character is scrutinized as a projection of racist attitudes in the author and his period of history.

Doctor Robinson robs graves and has enlisted Muff Potter and Injun Joe to accompany him to the cemetery. Years ago he shunned Injun Joe at a moment of perceived need, and the latter, who has been holding a grudge against him, takes advantage of a scuffle among the three men to stab the doctor to death. The murder is involuntarily witnessed by Huck and Tom, an event that changes the rest of their lives.

Muff Potter, the hapless and innocent instrument of Injun Joe's conniving, is saved from his fate by Tom's testimony in court.

Widow Douglas, a wealthy and good-hearted citizen, lives atop Cardiff Hill. Her late husband's past actions generate revengeful impulses in Injun Joe, which he intends to take out on her. Past kind deeds to Huck Finn inspire Huck to initiate a rescue attempt that saves her. She sees good in every "creature of the Lord's," even in Huck.

Welchman Jones and his brawny sons come to the rescue of the widow Douglas after Huck frantically appeals for their help. Animated by plain decency and a democratic spirit, Welchman Jones later befriends and cares for Huck.

Summary and Analysis

Chapter 1

A few lines into *The Adventures of Tom Sawyer* the reader senses
that the village of St. Petersburg would be quieter, slower, and
less interesting without Tom Sawyer in its midst. His presence is
urgently sought after in the first line: "Tom!" His first appearance
is a blur of motion; he outsmarts his Aunt Polly and disappears.
He escapes punishment for his first act of mischief—stealing jam
out of one of his aunt's carefully prepared jars. Aunt Polly's reac-
tions to Tom's wayward conduct and disappearing acts demonstrate both her dependence on order, duty, and discipline for her
own sense of stability and her unsteady vacillation between her
conscience and her heart. The former urges her to punish Tom;
the latter breaks when she does. This uneasy dynamic between
aunt and nephew repeats itself throughout the novel. These first
aunt/nephew interactions reveal another repeating pattern in the
novel: Despite being chronically at odds with each other, they are
more bound by affection than exasperation.

Twain couples with Aunt Polly's righteous and hardworking
demeanor a few harmless hypocrisies. She has, for example,
a pair of phony glasses—her lensless "state" pair, Twain calls
them—that provide a bit of flair and pseudosophistication in
her otherwise pedestrian life.

Half brother Sid also makes his first appearance with a characteristic gesture: He tattles on Tom and acts smugly about it.
Tom vows to get revenge but is rerouted by escaping from the
house again, this time to practice whistling in private—a new
talent that gives him a "strong, deep, unalloyed pleasure." Tom,
it can be deduced, is easily pleased. This cheerfulness and the
charisma that comes with it potentially help him to get others
to do his work for him; he entertains Jim, "the small colored
boy" working for the family, with his stories while Jim chops
both their shares of the evening's wood supply.

Tom meets the "new boy in town," who, like him in age and
size, is entirely unlike him in every other way, a true anomaly,

a "dandy," dressed up (in Tom's eyes) as if for a fancy weekend event on a mere weekday. Their encounter—circling around, eyeing each other, and muttering verbal threats—is reminiscent of two insecure dogs meeting for the first time. The boy, both threat and curiosity to Tom with his "citified air . . . that ate into Tom's vitals," issues a few too many dares for Tom to ignore, and the rivals finally resort to violence, now "[gripping] together like [fighting] cats." Tom, victorious, leaves, but not before the new boy throws a rock at him and runs home. For the second time in less than a day, Tom vows revenge. (Tom's promises of revenge are rarely fulfilled; serious acts of revenge in the novel are carried out by truly sinister characters.) Sneaking into his room through the window, Tom falls into Aunt Polly's trap; as punishment, she tells Tom, he must spend his free Saturday doing hard labor.

Chapter I concludes with Twain asserting, "[Tom Sawyer] was not the Model Boy of the village," a remark the reader suspects is an understatement.

Chapter II

Tom's hard labor requires whitewashing 30 yards of a 9-foot-high fence—the famous chore associated with Mark Twain, its image used for many purposes, including advertising for paint companies. The task—or Tom's contemplation of having to do it—and the thought of the "delicious expeditions" he'd thought up for himself that day bring on a "deep melancholy." The appearance of Jim on his way to the town pump initiates the strategic thinking that Tom often employs in order to get others to do his chores for him. Aunt Polly has already anticipated Tom's tricks and briefly outsmarts him by showing up and swatting Jim, who has almost succumbed to Tom's wiles. The war of wits between aunt and nephew—a major theme in the novel—continues when Aunt Polly leaves and Tom, drawing on "psychology" from the mind of the narrator, cleverly gets not only the satisfaction of seeing his entire task completed by other boys but by boys willing to give up their little "treasures" for the privilege of doing it. Twain's zany humor is evident in his description of Tom's first "victim," his friend Ben

Rogers, barreling noisily down the street pretending to be a steamboat (the "Big Missouri"), the steamboat captain, and the engine bells, all at the same time.

The author shares this observation about Tom:

> He had discovered a great law of human action, without knowing it—namely, that in order to make a man or a boy covet a thing, it is only necessary to make the thing difficult to obtain. If he had been a great and wise philosopher, like the writer of this book, he would now have comprehended that Work consists of whatever a body is *obliged* to do, and that Play consists of whatever a body is not obliged to do.

Whatever merit this observation has in regard to the psychology of human motivation, it seems unlikely to have originated in the brain of Tom Sawyer. It is an example of what critics call Twain's "narrative intrusions"; the novel has many of these, and the reader decides whether to be amused or annoyed by them.

Chapter III

Small ironies abound in this chapter. Tom, already rewarded with Ben's partially chewed apple, receives another from Aunt Polly as she, with astonished pleasure, rejoices over Tom's accomplishment of not one but three coats of whitewashing. Heavy moralizing accompanies every gesture of Aunt Polly, it seems; this time she tells her duplicitous nephew that the apple should be enjoyed all the more because it rewards both virtue and hard work. Undeserving of such a reward, Tom steals a doughnut when she is not looking and flees—guilt free—into the rest of the day's adventures.

Tom escapes to the first of dozens of imaginative and self-generated pastimes that he and his companions will enjoy throughout the novel—adventures made all the more exciting by being utterly free of any adult supervision. In this instance, Tom and his best friend, Joe Harper, organize their companions into two groups of soldiers who enact a battle scene complete with a pre-established *casus belli*, an accounting of the dead, and exchange of prisoners. By his own account, Mark Twain spent many years of his own childhood at just this sort of play. In a letter to childhood friend Will Bower, Twain falls into a rapture of nostalgia remembering all their antics:

" . . . you had the measles & I went to your house purposely to catch them"; "we stole [Jimmy Finn's] dinner while he slept in the vat & fed it to the hogs in order to keep them still till we could mount them & have a ride"; and "[we played] Robin Hood in our shirt-tails, with lath swords, in the woods on Holliday's Hill on those long summer days" (Norton edition, ed. Clark, 191–92).

Twain excels at evoking summertime pleasures, scents, pastimes, and leisure. The dusty roadways, gardens, hideouts, and swimming holes in the Mississippi River are almost as palpably rendered as well.

The day continues—an almost perfect string of happy events for Tom. In true adolescent style, he falls instantly out of one love into another. The "new" girl is Becky Thatcher, but until he learns her name, she is the "Adored Unknown"; the "old" girl is Amy Lawrence. While Tom is realizing that his passion for Amy was "only a poor little evanescent partiality," he throws himself into gymnastic poses and stunts to show off for Becky, who throws him a pansy for his efforts. Smitten, Tom heads home, where not even being blamed for Sid's breaking the sugar bowl and getting unfairly smacked by Aunt Polly can lessen his giddiness and delight.

Twain is obviously having fun with his story, but as G.K. Chesterton observed, the author's wit is sometimes like a sword with a painful point. Aunt Polly in this scene has made an error of judgment and acts righteously to inflict punishment, but her righteousness evaporates the moment she realizes she might have erred but cannot admit it because "discipline forbade that." More satire is introduced as Tom indulges in the "luxury" of self-pity while imagining his aunt discovering that she has punished the wrong boy. Still in the grip of his self-dramatizing, he deliberately avoids association with anything cheery; when his kind (and cheerful) cousin Mary arrives, he quickly leaves so he can prolong his "dismal felicity." This effusively romantic chapter ends when Tom, swooning under the window he imagines looks into Becky's bedroom, hears some unkind words from the housemaid and has a bucket of water dumped onto his prostrate body.

Chapter IV

An amusing description of a boy taking a bath without getting clean is found in this chapter: "the clean territory stopped short at his chin and jaws . . . beyond this . . . was a dark expanse of unirrigated soil. . . ." The reason for the bath is that it is Sunday—the day of cleanliness, godliness, virtue, and, for Tom and other poor families, the wearing of the "other clothes." Aunt Polly delivers her own Sunday morning lesson, and his cousin Mary affectionately bribes Tom into memorizing his Bible verses. Decked out feeling "exceedingly improved and uncomfortable," Tom heads to Sunday school accompanied by Sid and Mary who are actually looking forward to the day's events.

Mark Twain's relationship to church, Christianity, and religion in general was not clear cut. Sometime in 1874 he read W.E.H. Lecky's *History of European Morals from Augustus to Charlemagne* (1869) and recorded these contradictory responses for all to later read: "If I have understood this book aright, it proves two things beyond shadow or question: 1: That Christianity is the very invention of Hell itself; 2 and that Christianity is the most precious and elevating and ennobling boon ever vouchsafed to the world" (Howard Baetzhold, *Mark Twain and John Bull: The British Connection* 138). Twain's earliest experiences in church produced both dread and awe, and, like Tom, he grew up in a family that expected children to achieve righteous conformity by memorizing a certain number of Bible verses. Twain grew away from that influence and had, like so many believers during these times, to absorb the implication of Darwin's discoveries. His religious faith itself evolved, but he never completely discredited faith or the church. He remained, however, steadfastly vocal about the corrupting influence of money on morality and the manifold manifestations of religious hypocrisy and self-righteousness. In *Tom Sawyer*, Twain is clearly enjoying his satirical treatment of the church which, especially in Chapter IV, seems to reward pomposity, ignorance, and meaningless recitations.

Tom's efforts at memorization are motivated solely by Mary's bribe, but Tom is after larger gains: He tricks his Sunday school companions into trading him the "tickets" they have earned for each memorized verse in exchange for whatever random items he has accumulated in his pockets from his tricks on the same boys the day before. After maneuvering his way through the maze of ticket exchanges and values, he—improbably—ends up with the highest number and is poised for his great reward.

Superintendent Walters then goes from the moment of speaking in an ordinary manner to suddenly speaking with feigned gravity and holiness. Even the superintendent's shoes reflect his pretentions and the importance he places in appearance; their turned-up tips are formed by being held pressed against a wall for hours. The occasion for this performance is the arrival of church visitors: the especially "prodigious personage," Judge Thatcher, his wife, and young Becky. Their arrival sets off the bustle of activities: Mr. Walters and the church librarian fall into a meaningless scurrying about; the teachers, ready to smack their pupils for every gesture not in perfect conformity with their notions of righteous behavior, suddenly turn appreciative and adoring when their superiors show up; and Tom starts little fights and makes faces to get Becky's attention. Twain calls this phony posturing on the part of the adults "showing off," and its purpose in the novel, besides amusement, is to remind the reader that it really is not Tom's fault that he is uninspired by the adults in the community and the example they set: Their pretensions are surely counterproductive to anything useful or inspiring that might come from reading the Bible.

The chapter concludes with Tom poised to experience a moment of self-glorification that does not end well for him and is too embarrassing for the author to relate. It has to do with mistaking the Old Testament David and Goliath for one of the New Testament apostles.

Chapter V

Many notable townspeople make their appearances in church on this same Sunday morning, among them Aunt Polly; the doddering postmaster; the "unnecessary" major; the intriguing widow Douglas, the belle of the village with her "simpering admirers" in tow; Willie Mufferson, Tom's nemesis, who hovers around his mother "as if she were cut glass"; and all the "ill-bred" members of the church choir. The visitors to the Sunday school, were, by contrast, not townspeople. They live several miles away, a distance to the townspeople that seems like "the other side of the world" and a reminder of what "provincial" meant at that time in the nineteenth century.

Twain's keen eye, always roving about during his own churchgoing years, makes note of the strange verbal intonations used to deliver the sermon and the curious tradition of inserting into the program of worship a long list of announcements—secular and otherwise. He writes, "Often, the less there is to justify a traditional custom, the harder it is to get rid of it."

A fly landing on the back of the pew in the middle of the too-long prayer rescues Tom from the burden of having to listen. Tom's interactions with the fly and the antics that follow rescue the entire congregation from the same fate. In Twain's memory apparently, the best part of the morning service in this particular town and time is when it comes to an end.

The incident involving Tom, the vagrant poodle, and the pinch-bug has generated a lot of critical commentary. It brings much "unholy mirth" to such a bored and enervated crowd. Critic Judith Fetterley writes:

> The world of St. Petersburg is dull and sleepy, and its arch enemy is the boredom which lies at its heart, making it so sensation-hungry that everything that happens is greeted as an entertainment. . . . The world of St. Petersburg is trapped into boredom by its own hypocrisy, by its refusal to admit how dull and uninteresting the

things which it professes to value really are. It is against this background that Tom's centrality to St. Petersburg can be understood. He provides life, interest, amusement; he is a master entertainer with a bug for every occasion. ("The Sanctioned Rebel," Norton Critical Edition 280)

Chapter VI

School is the next challenge—so tedious that Tom wishes for the unpleasant symptoms of colic in order to avoid it. His little deceptions do not fool Aunt Polly, however, and Tom is left with no good excuse to miss school and the potential presented by a prematurely extracted tooth. Irrepressible, on his way to school he makes use of the new gap in his mouth to show off a new spitting technique—a feat so dramatic that he quickly upstages all the other boys and their tricks.

Before reaching school, Tom encounters Huckleberry Finn, the "juvenile pariah of the village," the only resident unattached to any kind of authority "[who] came and went, at his own free will" and was scorned by alarmed mothers and worshipped by the children. Twain sums up (somewhat disingenuously): "In a word, everything that goes to make life precious, that boy had."

The arrival of Huck Finn in the story introduces some of the most colorful aspects of small-town, backwoods life: the various myths, legends, superstitions (dead cats cure warts) and gossip. Huck also introduces to the narrative the first mention of darker aspects and elements, as talk of witches and other socially harmful entities become part of this otherwise amusing scene. The boys part for the day secure in a plan that will take them to a cemetery and a possible encounter with the devil itself.

The chapter ends with two minor classroom melodramas. The first is the thrashing Tom receives for being late to school, despite his decision to give a truthful excuse; the second is the "punishment" of being put with the girls, in conveniently close proximity to Becky Thatcher, who all too quickly succumbs to his charms. In short, for Tom, this is more reward than punishment.

Chapter VII

Tom teams up with Joe Harper to fend off classroom boredom by playing tricks on a bug. The earlier scene in the church exposes a similar disregard for the suffering of other creatures. These attitudes are often components reflective of adolescent narcissism; again, readers may choose to find them amusing or disturbing. One obvious reading of this scene is that the tick is a stand-in for Tom. Critic L. Moffitt Cecil writes:

> . . . Mark Twain has shaped [the novel's earliest] events in such a way that readers cannot miss the point of the tick-running. Imaginative, energetic, venturesome Tom is shown to be in constant conflict with the village authority represented by the home, the church, the school. Each of these three institutions in turn is seen trying to curb Tom's natural exuberance and make him conform to the village notion of a good boy. (Cecil, "Tom Sawyer: Missouri Robin Hood." *Collected Essays* 113–14)

The schoolmaster's "tremendous thwack" on their shoulders and the noontime break bring these exploits to an end. Tom uses his lunchtime to hide out with Becky, and the two, who know little about love, nonetheless freely declare eternal love to each other. In a matter of moments, however, Becky goes into a brief swoon after learning Tom has been previously "engaged." Not even his proffered brass knob can undo this romantic wound. Tom disappears, and Becky becomes inconsolable.

Chapter VIII

The capriciousness of "true love" has apparently unsettled Tom and distracted him from his usual pursuits. He skips the rest of his school day and heads at "a moody jog" toward the summit of Cardiff Hill. Safe in his pleasant solitude, Tom falls into a melancholy state and wishes he could figure out how to die—dramatically, but only "temporarily." He rescues himself from this gloomy mood through three playful fantasies: disappearing "beyond the seas" never to return; disappearing to become a soldier, returning "all war-torn and illustrious"; and disappearing to join the Indians for the excitement of hunting buffalo and going into battle, returning as a gloriously befeathered and "hideously painted" chief to stun and amaze his Sunday school companions with "blood-curdling war hoop[s]." In his imagination, at least, Tom, the imprisoned insect, has escaped his confining boundaries.

At no time is Tom really alone in his fantasies: He has an audience of at least one imagined onlooker (Becky) who—herself feeling melancholy back at school—is awaiting his return. Desiring more of an audience, Tom gets carried away in his ultimate fantasy of becoming a pirate, one so romantically audacious that "his name would fill the world and make people shudder!"

Tom is jolted back to reality when one of his favorite superstitions does not work (one lost marble cannot be given powers to draw all lost marbles to its hiding place). He is joined by Joe and, together, they play, embodying characters from the story of Robin Hood (one of Mark Twain's favorite pastimes from his own youth). Neither boy puts much value in classroom learning, but they devoutly go "by the book" when acting out their Robin Hood adventures. When Joe strays from the text, Tom abruptly brings him back. Of this play, Cecil writes:

> Tom's hero worship [of Robin Hood] goes far beyond mere idle adulation, mere playacting. Subconsciously at least he identifies with Robin Hood: he recognizes a correlation between the world of St. Petersburg and Robin's England, and he takes the initiative, as Robin had done centuries before, to oppose or circumvent the well-meaning, though too often self-defeating, village tyrannies. (115)

It is observations like these that many critics summon in suggesting that Twain's purpose in writing *Tom Sawyer*, aside from providing entertainment, was to promote a subversive view of some of the ways society organizes itself. The assumption of good intentions on the part of village elders toward the next generation is not so much questioned as it is shown to be sensationally ineffective at achieving the desired results.

The chapter ends with an idyllic scene of children at play, each cooperating with the other to ensure the continuation of a favored pastime. The boys lament that there are not more outlaws for them to roust, and Twain reports: "They . . . would rather be outlaws a year in Sherwood Forest than President of the United States forever."

Chapter IX

Throughout the novel we see Tom living by his senses. In this chapter, it is his sense of sound that is foregrounded. Before he escapes into the night to visit the cemetery with Huck and his dead cat, he lies awake, and then half-awake, and takes in one by one the summer nighttime sounds of old wood creaking, a ticking clock otherwise muffled by daytime noises, a distant dog's howl, and the solitary cricket that always seems to be about three inches from your ear.

Some critics and readers have questioned the appropriateness of inserting into a story for children the horrifying scene of the revengeful murder of Dr. Robertson by Injun Joe that occurs in this chapter. Others have pointed out that standards for nineteenth-century children's literature would not have prevented it. In "Juvenile Literature," Linda A. Morris refers to Francis Molson's essay in *Touchstones: Reflections on the Best in Children's Literature* (1985), in which he argues that Twain's novel embodies 12 of 13 standards for good children's literature, specifically, "an 'opportunity to experience known dangers vicariously' and [the inclusion of] 'various threats and promises which correspond to children's basic fears and hopes'" (*A Companion to Mark Twain* 374). It was perhaps fitting in Twain's mind to begin a chapter that ends in a gruesome scene with nighttime musings that sometimes soothe and sometimes stir up imaginary fears in a child's mind.

The cemetery with its "crazy board fence [that] stood upright nowhere" has long ago relinquished its purpose for remembering the dead with customary dignity. With pretensions of dread the boys anticipate their planned sighting of the devil and then are seized with real terror at the sight of mere humans approaching, animated by their own mysterious and menacing agenda. The boys recognize the voices of Muff Potter, the town drunk; Injun Joe, "that murderin' half-breed"; and Dr. Robinson, who, for his own nefarious purposes, robs a freshly laid grave. In this pivotal scene, the boys are not actors but witnesses to a grim drama involving duplicity, extortion, revenge, murder, and betrayal. The grave-robbing doctor is stabbed to death as Injun Joe announces he has "settled a score," and the wrong man is convinced that he is responsible and feels remorse. The boys, who saw what really happened, have long fled.

Injun Joe, looking down on the dead doctor and what his violence has wrought, says: "I swore I'd get even with you if it took a hundred years. . . . The Injun blood ain't in me for nothing. . . ." These words have generated the most substantive critical discussions about *Tom Sawyer*, registering, as they starkly do, the pervasive prejudices held at that time by the author himself.

Chapter X

In a safe place far from the scene of the crime, Huck and Tom slowly regain their equilibrium by comparing what each has just witnessed. Injun Joe's vague associations with menace, hinted at earlier in the novel, have suddenly turned from titillating to terrifying. This new threat is both real and grave; the boys' fate is in his hands and, were they to publicly expose his complicity in the murder and Injun Joe escaped hanging for the crime, they know he "wouldn't make any more of drownding [them] than [he would] a couple of cats." After some amusing speculation on drunkenness and its various manifestations, the boys decide on a strategy for dealing with the "deep, and dark, and awful" dilemma they are facing: a handwritten oath (a handshake being insufficient for the gravity of the situation), signed with their ritualistically extracted blood, proclaiming that "Huck Finn and Tom Sawyer [swear] they will keep mum about this and they wish they may drop down dead in their tracks if they ever tell and rot."

A dog's "lugubrious howl" brings on another "agony of fright"; both think they are about to die and commence to list petty sins that each fears will be sufficient to send them to hell. The howling turns out to be provoked by Muff Potter, recently introduced in the cemetery scene, drunk and passed out nearby. The boys head home, "cogitating."

The next morning Tom discovers that his "virtuous" brother has deceived and tattled on him again, but instead of corporal punishment, he endures the much more difficult-to-bear consequence of having to watch Aunt Polly's emotional collapse over her despair of ever getting Tom to do anything right. Miserable with guilt, he heads to school, receives a flogging with Joe for having skipped school the day before, and is greeted with even more misery—the sight of his brass knob returned to his desk, a discouraging sign that his romance with Becky Thatcher will be short lived.

Chapter XI

The invention of the telegraph, observes the narrator, would not have shortened the time it took for news of Doctor Robinson's murder to spread around town. School is canceled, as if for a holiday, and all the townspeople head for the cemetery. Muff Potter, drunk, confused, and not the actual criminal, has returned to the scene of the crime, acting like a criminal. Tom and Huck watch with fear as Potter's fate is sealed by Injun Joe's incriminating words. When Joe is not instantly struck down by a heavenly lightning bolt, the boys know he is in alliance with the devil. With this realization, all thoughts of championing justice, following their consciences, and telling the truth about the murderer's true identity are abandoned, but the boys' fascination with the devil and desire to lay their own eyes on him remain undiminished.

This chapter bears the expected mark of comedy (the reader laughs at the odd antics and juxtapositions and the mock-heroic language used by Twain to describe them) but at the same time most of these scenes portray human weaknesses, stupidity, avarice, duplicity, and preoccupation with concerns no more noble than mere self-preservation. One minor exception is that Tom's conscience reasserts itself in his nightmares; he is fearful, but he also knows an evil deed has been done. Sid reports on

Tom's disturbed nighttime ramblings and is on the verge of tormenting his brother with interpretations of his words when both Mary and Aunt Polly intervene with confessions of their own nighttime disturbances. Sid remains on guard, however, perhaps sensing his brother has access to nefarious and exciting mysteries that he is missing out on. The reader never sees anything resembling compassionate concern in Sid's wily behavior.

The town responds to its shock by escalating its animosity for Injun Joe, yet not because he is believed to be guilty. Briefly, the townspeople consider subjecting Joe to the instruments of torture known as "tar and feathering" and "[riding] him on a rail," but they are deterred by their fear of his "formidable" character. In contrast, Tom responds with genuine compassion for the hapless Muff Potter, sneaking items of "small comfort" to him through the grated jail window. Overall, the chapter does not present an uplifting view of humanity.

Chapter XII

Tom falls into a state of despondent ennui after Becky temporarily disappears from the life of the town. She is said to be ill, and with characteristic adolescent overreaction, Tom torments himself with thoughts of her possible impending death. Aunt Polly is alarmed, and, like Twain's own mother, Jane Clemens, and the majority of nineteenth-century housewives, she looks to one of several patented medicines that promise cures for all sorts of ailments, sometimes "miraculously." In an essay in the Norton Critical Edition, K. Patrick Ober discusses the secret ingredient of these "cure-alls":

> The popularity of the Pain-Killer and similar patented medicines was undoubtedly related to their considerable content of alcohol, just as the widespread appeal of other patent medicines was due to their opiate content. Information about the content of the different patent medicines was not typically shared with the general public, as the trademark on the medicines allowed their manufacturing process and contents to be kept secret. However, there can be little question that the secret

ingredients of the patented medicines contributed greatly to their appeal. For example, the fact that Shiloh's Cure for Consumption was fortified with heroin undoubtedly broadened its market to include many citizens who were not consumptive. (Norton Critical Edition 210)

Twain's relationship with his mother was affectionate and mainly harmonious, but one can get a sense of what he must have endured as a child in his description of Aunt Polly's "feverish" enthusiasms for the cure of the moment:

> She was a subscriber for all the "Health" periodicals . . . [and all] the "rot" they contained about ventilation, and how to go to bed, and how to get up, and what to eat, and what to drink, and how much exercise to take, and what frame of mind to keep one's self in, and what sort of clothing to wear, was all gospel to her, and she never observed that her health-journals of the current month customarily upset everything they had recommended the month before.

Despite Aunt Polly's elaborate efforts, Tom remains "as dismal as a hearse." A new medicine, called simply "Pain-killer," is tried, and, since it has an effect on the patient said to be similar to that of having a fire set beneath him, she is persuaded of its efficacy and lets him have it whenever he pleases. Her laxity leads to a predictable outcome; Tom uses the stuff for unintended purposes: attempting to patch the floor cracks by letting the supply drip incrementally through them, and healing the cat by pouring a teaspoonful down its throat. The cracks survive, but the cat goes into wild gyrations, sending flowerpots and furniture in all directions. Tom dampens his aunt's zeal for miracle medicines by pointing out that what is cruel to the cat might also be fairly judged to be cruel to the boy. Laughter appears to have healed his gloomy spirits, and he heads back to school, where he is overjoyed to see Becky returned to class. He is then instantly dismayed, however, to discover she continues to have no interest in him.

Chapter XIII

"Gloomy and desperate . . . forsaken [and] friendless," Tom decides his only chance for excitement is to run away from home and take up a life of crime. He nonetheless cannot resist indulging in some egotistical imaginings of how he would be missed by those he is leaving behind. He even experiences a brief spasm of nostalgia for the sounds of the school bell, which he will "never, never" hear again.

The plan involves Joe who, Tom learns, is experiencing his own version of being fed up with life and was just then heading to propose a similar adventure to Tom. What they plan—and Huck Finn will join them—is the first real adventure of the novel, involving the theft of provisions, a midnight rendezvous, a trip on the Mississippi River, an uninhabited island, and a great expanse of "unpeopled forest." In addition, adding even more appeal to the plan, was the delicious anticipation of being at the center of the town's frantic attention once everyone has discovered their disappearance.

The vignettes that follow of the three boys on the raft loyally playacting the tales of piracy Tom has memorized are uplifting reminders of the delight to be had in camaraderie and play. Tom, Huck, and Joe, with their new identities and their playful adventures, are not seeking material gain, favorable status, or power over anyone. There is, instead, the pursuit of fun for its own sake, a lot of self-dramatizing and posturing, and always the possibility of surprise.

In the middle of the night, they make their planned landing, secure their provisions, make a fire, and prepare to sleep, like the "outlaws" they have become, unprotected, under the stars. Some combination of the nighttime sounds, a full stomach, and the almost inconceivable prospect of being truly free bring all three boys to a reverent pause. The reader watches as they inhabit this adventure of their own conjuring and feel pure contentment in the experience of just being alive. At the same time and perhaps more important, the narrator affords the boys the ability of being aware of themselves and their good fortune. Here, they exult, they can leave behind "all that blame foolishness" of their former lives; they can skip school with impunity;

and no one can "come and pick at" them or "bullyrag" them. They are content, especially Huck, who is having the rare experience of falling asleep with a full stomach. "I don't want nothing better'n this," he says.

Not quite as content, Tom and Joe are visited by their troubled consciences that disturb their peace by reminding them they have stolen provisions earlier in the day. These two fall asleep less like pirates than like confused little boys who are not quite sure what they are up to.

Chapter XIV

Tom awakes in an Edenlike world, ensconced in nature in its most benign form. A tiny inchworm comes into view bringing to Tom's superstitious mind a promise that a new suit of clothes—appropriate to a pirate's life—is coming his way. Other tiny members of the natural world pass by him, purposefully engaged. For these brief moments, life is in harmony with itself, and Tom is "at home."

Nature provides sustenance as well. From the river, the boys catch fish to go with their bacon. Their contentment is so complete that the discovery that their raft has come unmoored and floated off does not cause any alarm. Similarly, the sight of the village across the river does not provoke any feelings of longing or remorse. Jackson's Island—3 miles long and ¼ mile wide, they discover—is their utopia. When they are not exploring, swimming in the Mississippi River, or eating, the boys are at rest.

After this spate of euphoria, the boys notice "[a] sort of undefined longing [creeping] upon them." They are experiencing homesickness, of course, but none dares confess it aloud. They are distracted by intermittent sounds of a cannon being fired; and, after rallying to attention and wishing themselves at the scene of whatever disaster is at hand, they surmise that someone has drowned. After speculating about the intellectual and spiritual capability of "an ignorant lump of bread," the boys realize with a shock that it is their own townspeople out on the river trying to raise the boys' presumably drowned bodies. This discovery prompts the boys to gloat; they are in their favorite location again—at the center of everyone's attention. During the night (when conscience seems most likely to emerge), it occurs to Tom and Joe that their happy adventure as pirates on an island might not be as much fun for those back onshore worried about them. While the others sleep, Tom makes a plan.

Chapter XV

This chapter depicts acts of prowess (Tom's upstream swimming) and intrigue (leaving messages on pieces of bark, sneaking a ride on the ferry's skiff, and spying) and a gesture simultaneously sweet and maniacally narcissistic (Tom watching his family mourn his "death" and deciding to leave Aunt Polly a kiss but no reassuring sign of his continuing existence). The breadth of Twain's imagination is on full display.

Overhearing himself and Joe lamented and praised almost moves Tom to reveal himself, but the prospect of extending the melodramatic ruse—with all its "theatrical gorgeousness"—a bit longer is too tempting for Tom to resist. He leaves no sign of his presence and disappears into the darkness, back to the river and the island, where Huck is expressing doubts about his integrity as a pirate and Joe is reassuring him Tom's integrity is intact.

Chapter XVI

The American landscape has been more than a background for American writers. Its power, beauty, capacity to provide an almost infinite-seeming source of sustenance both nutritional and spiritual, its capacity to provide solace and danger and to inspire adventurousness has made it almost a character in itself. At the top of any reader's list are Melville's ocean, Hawthorne's deep northern woods, Faulkner's deep southern woods, Sarah Orne Jewett's piney hills, and Thoreau's Walden Pond.

For Mark Twain, the best and the worst features of America are represented by the Mississippi River. A romanticized waterway associated with exploration and expansion, it is also the site of commerce, of the ravages and benefits of American capitalism, and, in Twain's era, the boundary between slave and nonslave states.

In this chapter, the reader experiences both the river and the fictional Jackson's Island, uninhabited and densely wooded, located about 3 miles downriver from St. Petersburg. American studies professor Leo Marx, writing about the American landscape, calls Jackson's Island, which figures prominently in both *Tom Sawyer* and *Huckleberry Finn*, "another of those enchanting pastoral oases so endlessly fascinating to the American imagination" (*The Machine in the Garden*, 326). Critic Andrew Dix, in his essay "Twain and the Mississippi," analyzes what he calls "the politics of swimming in [Twain's] work" (*A Companion to Mark Twain* 298). He begins by citing the passage from this chapter describing the boys swimming in the river on the day after Tom made his secret trip back to town. It is a sensual and idyllic scene:

> After breakfast they went whooping and prancing out on the bar, and chased each other round and round, shedding clothes as they went, until they were naked, and then continued the frolic far away up the shoal water of the bar, against the stiff current, which latter tripped their legs from under them from time to time and greatly increased the fun. And now and then they stooped in a group and splashed water in each other's faces with their palms, gradually approaching each other, with averted faces to avoid the strangling sprays and finally gripping and struggling till the best man ducked his neighbor, and then they all went under in a tangle of white legs and arms and came up blowing, sputtering, laughing and gasping for breath at one and the same time. (*Companion* 298)

One element to be noticed in this scene are the white arms and legs. Luxurious and unsupervised pleasures like these were not available to most black Americans then. In addition, after the boys' playful antics, they can run out of the water and "sprawl on the hot, white sand" and then, when they feel like it, go back into the river. Dix, in his essay, examines the contrast between utopian values and commercial ones associated with the Mississippi. His assessments are based on more of Twain's work than this early novel about boys growing up, but he makes this valuable observation:

> The boys in *Tom Sawyer* . . . alternate energetic swimming with periods of indolence by the river. Such "loafing" and "lazying" . . . has an ambiguous political value. If it is indeed a form of (non)motion opposed to the corporeal discipline required by a capitalistic productive mode, then its critical potential is compromised by its also expressing a kind of social privilege. . . . [Even] the outcast Huck is placed quite advantageously in Mississippi culture. If we look again at the group of swimmers, we see strict limits on precisely whose bodies can circulate in and around the water. The group is not only all-male, but also racially coded as "a tangle of white legs and arms." Any utopian sense of play upon the Mississippi is vitiated by this exclusion of female and African-American subjects. . . . (*A Companion to Mark Twain* 299)

After a time, despite the encompassing rhythms of play and relaxing, the first signs of serious discontent begin to surface. Joe is too homesick to deny it and is not dissuaded by promises of more swimming. Twain, the clever narrator, has Joe discover the perplexing phenomenon of losing interest in an exciting activity if part of the pleasure comes from its being forbidden. He gets some unkindly mocking from Tom and Huck as they watch him wade into the river heading home. Presently, Huck caves in too, citing loneliness, which Joe's departure has just made worse. Tom struts along the shore defiantly protecting his brave pirate identity as the "Black Avenger of the Spanish Main," while the mutineers, Huck (the "Red-Handed") and Joe (the "Terror of the Seas") abandon camp and the adventure. This strutting of Tom's, like most foolish acts of pride, comes to an end with the realization that his great plan—conceived while overhearing the plans for their funeral—will be ruined the moment the deserters reach home. Disclosing his secret plan is his last option and final seduction, and it proves effective. The three boys turn back to adventuring until the ideal moment for Tom to carry off his "stupendous plan" of arriving just in time to participate in their own funeral, presents itself.

They fill their time with little adventures. Learning to smoke a pipe following Huck's instructions starts them off and leads to posturing and boasting until the scene ends in a predictably comical way. Two formidable challenges are set before them. The first is a spectacular thunderstorm that drenches them and their imperfect shelter, sends them bolting into the woods when lightning threatens, and comes close to killing them with a falling sycamore tree. They rally and cope; they face their challenge and display the ability to endure out in the wild. The second challenge is boredom—how to fill the hours until the anticipated departure. This challenge they meet, as well, by simply changing their imaginative scenario from being pirates to being Indians. As enemy chieftains, they scalp one another and others "by the thousands" and have a gory and, consequently, "extremely satisfying [day]." Even more satisfying for Tom and Joe, they later discover they can smoke a pipe without getting so sick they have to flee into the woods to save face.

The narrator's tone in describing the boys and their adventures is a mix of delight and condescension, and it is sometimes obvious that he is having as much fun in his imaginings as the boys are in the adventures he has created for them. Like the author, Twain's boys rely on the power of imagination to entertain themselves in the middle of nowhere.

Chapter XVII

From the beginning of the novel, Tom has been anticipating the staging of a dramatic scene that comes to fruition in this chapter. In Chapter III, after his aunt has mistakenly punished him instead of Sid, the real culprit, for breaking a favorite sugar bowl, Tom pleasantly indulges in self-pity, picturing his remorseful aunt grieving not once but twice over her dead or dying nephew. Later in the same chapter, on the cold ground beneath Becky's bedroom window, he imagines her coming upon his lifeless body the next morning and shedding one little tear as she contemplates the injustice of "a bright young life so rudely blighted, so untimely cut down."

Whatever terms one chooses to use for and characterize this behavior—*showing off*, *adolescent narcissism*, or *self-glorification*—the novel abounds in it, a mode that has attracted much critical attention. In his introduction to the Oxford University Press 1993 edition of the novel, American literature scholar Lee Clark Mitchell talks about Tom's "flagrant exhibitionism," his readiness, like his author's, "[to be] perpetually on stage" (xvii). Recalling the first scene (Aunt Polly and the phony eyeglasses she uses for show, Tom's showing off his Sunday school tickets, the showing off prompted by the arrival of the Thatchers) Mitchell comments:

> The only mistake lies in seeing Tom as essentially different in this regard from anyone else in St. Petersburg, since everyone shares the same propensity as him. They are simply less successful. (xviii)

In this chapter, Tom upstages his earlier self-dramatizing fantasies by making an appearance at his own funeral and basking in the town's jubilant adoration. The town has prepared itself well for this stunning emotional release. Signs of ebbing vitality are everywhere. Everyone seems listless and absentminded. Memories of Tom and Joe help elevate the youths to heroic stature. Citizens fight for the distinction of having been the one to have last seen them alive. Having been beaten up by Tom has no distinction, because nearly everyone can make the same claim. With remorse, Becky mopes about not having saved the brass andiron knob "to remember [Tom] by."

The scene in the overflowing church is the same, only intensified. The minister misleads himself and everyone in the grieving congregation into recalling as noble certain mischievous deeds performed by the departed boys. Death has transformed little miscreants, small-town sociopaths, into angels. While everyone is drawn into the communal sadness, Tom, Joe, and Huck are preparing their entrance for the moment that is calculated to yield the greatest effect. Yet after the boys make their spectacular appearance and the great hymn is triumphantly sung, Tom notices one imperfection: No one rushes forward to welcome and embrace the outcast Huck, standing alone, "a ruin of drooping rags." This lapse is remedied by Aunt Polly whose effusive ministrations make Huck even more uncomfortable than when he was standing alone. Meanwhile, Tom stands luxuriating in what he "[confesses] in his heart . . . was the proudest moment of his life."

Chapter XVIII

Although special attentions are conferred on Tom the next day, the reader watches as the old annoyances creep back and Tom's rapscallion nature reasserts itself. Aunt Polly chides Tom about being inconsiderate and wonders aloud why he could not have left her a reassuring sign as a token of his affection for her. Tom actually did consider making just this gesture while he was spying on his family, but he chose to go for the most thrilling and dramatic dénouement over sparing his aunt her anguish. He claims, as consolation, to have had dreams about her while out on the island, but his aunt, quite properly, dismisses this substitute as nothing more than what a cat would do. Tom then adds to his own fun by pretending to have dreamed about the events he had actually witnessed on his clandestine visit home. With each new revelation of his gift for clairvoyance, both Tom's charisma and ego expand, and he is rewarded with another apple from Aunt Polly.

Tom returns to community life, replacing his prancing and skipping with a new "dignified swagger." He is the envy of all the boys in town with his "swarthy sun-tanned skin" and his "glittering notoriety"—treasures he "would not have parted with . . . for a circus." Telling his stories while "serenely" smoking a pipe puts Tom at "the very summit of glory," an elevation he is determined to inhabit without Becky Thatcher's affections. His resolve lasts only moments longer than his first sight of her; something inspires him to flirt provocatively with Amy to demonstrate his indifference to Becky. Becky counters with a feigned flirtation of her own—with Alfred Temple, a choice certain to vex Tom. He may be the town's miraculous survivor, but to Becky, Tom is still not "in the land of the living." Distracted and deposed, Tom inconsiderately dismisses Amy and then acts out an imaginary flogging of his hated rival. When the chapter ends, Becky has likewise abruptly dismissed Alfred Temple, but she is undecided about what to do with Tom.

Chapter XIX

His spirits sagging, Tom returns home to find that his aunt has unraveled his recent deception. His primary transgression is the social embarrassment he has caused his aunt when the story she smugly relayed to Mrs. Harper about Tom's supposed clairvoyance is refuted by Joe, her son, who knew the truth. It is not the actual lie but the damage to her social ego that is the graver offense to Polly. A tender exchange between nephew and aunt, about whether or not his declaration of wishing to spare her a longer spell of grief was sincere, then ensues. Discovering that it was, Aunt Polly is supremely comforted.

Chapter XX

Tom's spirits have been temporarily raised by the brief exchange of affection with his aunt, but they droop again when his surprise encounter with Becky outside the schoolhouse leads to her display of hotheadedness and offended pride. Tom, with his sense of chivalry, allows himself to wish for but not to act on his impulse to give Becky the trouncing she would receive if she were a boy.

Both are nonetheless in for a trouncing at the hands of Mr. Dobbins, their humorless and listless schoolmaster. What energy he possesses seems to be expressed mainly in his robustly administered punishments. A reminder of his unfulfilled desire to be a doctor instead of a schoolteacher is found in a book on human anatomy that he keeps locked in his desk drawer and brings out to peruse when nothing else is required of him in the classroom. Of all the little "urchins" willing to risk their own demise to get their hands on the teacher's secret book, it is Becky who catches sight of the unlocked drawer. In her first real spontaneous and self-directed action in the novel, she snatches the book and flips through the pages until she comes upon a colored drawing of "a human figure, stark naked." Tom then startles her, and she rips the page. Fearing a "whipping" (girls were apparently not spared corporal punishment), she falls back into her indignant and simpering poses, stomps her feet, and abruptly leaves. Tom's response is much more developed and compelling. He has theories, views, notions, and superstitions about nearly every aspect of human behavior and motivation—insight beyond his years—and, although his theories prove frequently to be wrong, his efforts to understand them are lively and entertaining.

There are to be two trouncings that day, and Tom—fully innocent of both misdeeds—takes both punishments in one, appearing to play the "noble fool." It is nonetheless hard to see exactly what might be genuinely noble about these gestures. The first punishment, for spilling ink on the spelling book, Tom assumes he is deserving of simply because he is so used to being guilty in the past. The second punishment he receives has the appearance of being motivated by chivalry but is also fully self-serving. The second flogging, however, is the harshest ever given by Mr. Dobbins for reasons the reader is left to ponder.

Tom, through all these machinations, has finally managed to win back Becky's affections. He goes to sleep that night rewarded with the sweet memory of her words: "Tom, how *could* you be so noble!"

Chapter XXI

Mark Twain's enthusiasm for social reform and his gift for parody, both abundantly apparent in the Sunday school episodes, come fully to life in this chapter. It is the end of the school year and time to show the parents and other community members what achievements have been made by the students under Mr. Dobbins's instruction. The illustration accompanying many editions of the novel shows a classroom bedecked with ivy bows and framed sayings on the walls. "Time flies," observes one; "The pen is mightier than the sword," declares another; "Industry Must Thrive," insists another, confidently. "Knowledge Is Power" seems to sum up these adult-sponsored messages aimed at the younger generation, especially those children not sufficiently motivated by the simple pleasures of learning new things. No evidence is given to suggest that any of the promised "knowledge and power" will issue from any of the "educational" achievements chosen for the evening's display, more evidence of Twain's satirical posturing.

The examples of the children's academic efforts, their speeches sometimes so verbose and convoluted, so strained with affected earnestness as to defy any reasonable interpretation, animate this section of the novel. One speech that goes on for a lengthy paragraph seems to convey only that a lot of wind was blowing. The centerpiece in this charade of a year's worth of "education" is the recitation of speeches by several young ladies, one of whom comes forward with a composition titled, somewhat vacantly, "Is This, Then, Life?" The first lines seem to consist of vague and inarticulate eruptions of gratitude for the beauty of life and the last lines—improbably, suddenly, and inexplicably—express a complete reversal of these same sentiments.

Tom Sawyer, with "fine fury and frantic gesticulation," throws himself into a spirited delivery of the "unquenchable and indestructible 'Give me liberty or give me death' speech," but his legs quake and he begins to choke with stage fright, bringing his efforts to an embarrassing conclusion. Not surprisingly for a chapter about inept teaching and unruly classrooms, the scene concludes with an elaborately executed practical joke on Mr. Dobbins, whose uninspired teaching; cruel, relentless, and ineffectual punishments; and overall unsuitability for the position he holds call out for revenge. With involuntary assistance from an unhappy and blindfolded cat, the students get revenge on their teacher, who may be a bit too foggy from alcohol consumption to know what hit him. It is then, at last, time for summer vacation.

Twain had, by this time in his career, expressed an interest in educational reform and was invited by a member of the House Committee on Colleges and Common Schools to visit a school. In a letter written in 1864, he described his impressions of a classroom recitation and some recent "improvements" in pedagogy:

The fashion of reading selections of prose and poetry remains the same; and so does the youthful manner of doing that sort of thing. Some pupils read poetry with graceful ease and correct expression, and others place the rising and falling inflection at measured intervals, as if they had learned the lesson on a "see-saw"; but then they go undulating through a stanza with such an air of unctuous satisfaction, that it is a comfort to be around when they are at it. . . . The compositions read to-day were as exactly like the compositions I used to hear read in our school . . . : the cutting to the bone of the subject with the very first gash, without any preliminary foolishness; the inevitable and persevering tautology; the brief, monosyllabic sentences (beginning, as a general thing, with the pronoun "I"). . . . ("Letter from Mark Twain: Miss Clapp's School," *Territorial Enterprise*, January 1864; reprinted in *The Adventures of Tom Sawyer*, Norton Critical Edition 198).

Chapter XXII

Tom learns the second of his "profound" life lessons when he joins the Order of Cadets of Temperance. Enticed by the prospect of showing off in the order's flamboyant colors at the anticipated funeral of ailing Judge Frazer, Tom vows to keep the rules and refrain from smoking, chewing, and profanity. The "new thing" he learns is that "to promise not to do a thing is the surest way in the world to make a body want to go and do that very thing." Going without proves too challenging, and the judge's health seems to be improving, so Tom leaves the group. By this time in the novel, we are familiar with the protagonist's charms and special powers, but in this chapter, he is finally outsmarted by someone else or, rather, by death itself. The judge dies just in time to foil Tom's plans. He consoles himself with his recovered freedoms, but the consolation is short lived as he discovers the reverse of his earlier lesson is true: The freedom to do what he wants renders the things he wants to do considerably less appealing.

Also less appealing than anticipated is the summer vacation itself. An impressive number of entertaining events—when considering what a drab and provincial community St. Petersburg is—present themselves, including a circus, a minstrel show, a phrenologist, a mesmerizer, and a visiting revivalist group. Each is an attraction that does not last. Parties with girls are deemed fun, but there are not enough of them. Becky is on vacation with her family. Rain spoils the Fourth of July parade.

While Tom is laid low with a bout of measles, his friends go to the revival meetings and "get religion." The whole town has been swept up by images of doom and strategies for salvation. Even Huck greets Tom with quoted scripture when Tom is out and about again, healed of his measles and looking for fun. Lonely and dismayed, Tom imagines that a furious thunderstorm striking the town has been sent to warn him of his own doom.

Shortly, however, everything returns to normal. Huck and Joe are eating stolen melons, and Jim Hollis is presiding over a trial of a cat that has murdered a bird. But beneath all the activity—disappointing or exciting, reverent or sinful—is the memory of Doctor Robinson's gruesome murder by the hand of Injun Joe.

Chapter XXIII

The trial of Muff Potter for the murder of Doctor Robinson consumes the townspeople and keeps Tom in a perpetual "cold shiver." Huck and Tom agree that Potter "ain't no account" but that he has never harmed anyone and once shared a fish with Huck. Guilt and sympathy combine to draw both boys to the prison, where they hope their mere presence will magically draw out the falsely accused. For readers not persuaded of the essential goodness of the boys' natures, the inability of Huck and Tom to dismiss their concerns for the hapless Muff Potter supports this position. They fail, however, to resolve their ethical dilemma. As much as they are tempted, they cannot bring themselves to act. Their second-best choice is to sneak little gifts of tobacco and matches through the cell window to the grateful prisoner. Their prolonged period of guilt and ethical tension is set against the unnamable fears they associate with Injun Joe and the secret about him they are carrying.

The trial commences; guilt is established, and there seems no hope for the accused, who is not helping his own case by claiming to be uncertain about his guilt or innocence. Tom is beset with both insomnia and dreams "full of horror." He hangs around the courthouse to learn what he can about the proceedings and invariably hears the distressing news that Injun Joe's evidence is prevailing and "poor Potter" is doomed. On the trial's pivotal day, witnesses against Potter are called, but, to the consternation of the townspeople, not one is cross-examined or called on his behalf until Tom, in a dramatic surprise, is called by the defense to testify. Hesitantly, and then more confidently, Tom tells the true story, no doubt relishing his return to the center of the town's attentions. A dramatic testimony brings on a dramatic response: Injun Joe flees the courtroom. What compels Tom to relate the truth in court remains another mystery for the reader to ponder.

Chapter XXIV

This chapter relays not the mysterious process by which Tom's conscience overruled his hesitation to testify but the more pedestrian fact that he did, finally, tell his story to the lawyer the night before.

By day, Tom, the town's "glittering hero," struts with glory, but at night he is tormented by dreams "infested" by Injun Joe. Huck suffers an even more severe consequence: Learning that Tom had violated their sacred oath to tell no one what they had seen," [his] confidence in the human race [had been] well nigh obliterated." Both boys know no peace; only the sight of Injun Joe's corpse will return them to a sense of calm. But there is no corpse and no sight of Joe either. Even the arrival of a St. Louis detective claiming to have a "clew" fails to make Tom feel secure.

Chapter XXV

Perhaps for this reason—the unresolved murder and the menacing threat of Injun Joe—Mark Twain decided to change the subject in the twenty-fifth chapter. Almost as if the murder and trial never happened, the reader rejoins the innocent adventuring of young boys in the countryside. Tom gets it into his head to embark on a treasure hunt. Huck, who has plenty of time on his hands and no money, is Tom's perfect companion for this plan. Tom explains to Huck his amusing theories about who hid the money and where it is to be found. Enthralled by the prospect of finding a "brass pot with a hundred dollars in it" or "a rotten chest full of di'monds," they head off. As they make their way, Huck explains his preference of dollars over diamonds, being not attracted by their association with kings who have "slathers of them" and confused by Tom's description of "a raft [of diamonds] hopping about [Europe]." Tom shocks and disappoints Huck when he announces his intention to get married but then consoles Huck with an invitation to move in with the married couple when the time comes.

The boys go from one site to the next, each time exerting themselves to sweaty exhaustion with no treasure to show for it. The last site—a "ha'nted house"—initiates a conversation about different ways of being terrified. Huck is more scared of ghosts than he is of dead people because the dead might frighten you by talking, "but they don't come sliding around in a shroud, when you ain't noticing, and peep over your shoulder all of a sudden and grit their teeth." The boys resolve to "take a chance" and approach the dreaded house until, overtaken by their fears, they back away and head toward the safety of home.

An important difference between Tom and Huck is briefly shown here in the discussion about what to do with the hidden treasure once it is found. Carefree (except when he is hungry) and unattached to social conventions and institutions, Huck plans to enjoy his share as he pleases and save none, while the more conventional Tom will buy things he wants but save some for getting married.

Chapter XXVI

Childhood imaginings turn into grave realities in this chapter. Huck, more hesitant than Tom about digging up hidden treasures, "suddenly" remembers the day is Friday the Thirteenth, and both boys, their ambitions guided by superstitions of all kinds, decide the day is an inauspicious one for their plans. A game of "noble fun"—playing Robin Hood in the forest—occupies the rest of the day.

They return to the haunted house the next day, its facade only slightly less menacing in the daylight. Venturing through "ragged and abandoned cobwebs" and ascending a "ruinous staircase," they arrive on the second floor—a daring move to a place of no retreat. A sudden noise puts them in "a misery of fear." The most dreaded outcome of their explorations—worse than the talking dead or shrouded ghosts that sneak up on you—is before them: Injun Joe and his partner in crime are hiding out in the haunted house. The boys, immobilized with fright, overhear the two men discuss their plans. Tom's theories about who buries treasure and why they do so come to life before their eyes; miraculously they watch as the criminals bury not one but two treasures. "Here was treasure-hunting under the happiest auspices—[no] bothersome uncertainty as to where to dig." Yet hidden riches are not their immediate concern. Joe catches on to the presence of others in the house—the ones who brought the tools just used to dig up one treasure and rebury two. With thoughts of some planned revenge in his mind, Joe takes off with the newly discovered box of money and temporarily parts company with his partner. The boys, fearing being the target of Joe's planned revenge, flee in a different direction, but not before taking in all the clues Joe has left about the still-buried treasure.

Chapter XXVII

In his 1993 introduction to *Tom Sawyer*, critic Lee Clark Mitchell made an observation about the novel that is especially applicable to these treasure-hunting episodes. He wrote, "Few authors have evoked as skillfully as Twain the wide-eyed state of childhood ignorance, revealing it as an unstable blend of confident innocence and fearful bewilderment" (xv). "Fearful bewilderment" seems to have crept over Tom during the night because the next day he is not even sure whether his and Huck's encounter with Joe and his "patch-eyed Spanish devil" was a dream or an actual event. Meeting up with Huck confirms that the adventure was real enough. The next challenge, then, becomes how to get some of the treasure for themselves. Tom comes up with an idea and takes off without Huck because, the narrator explains, town rebel and rascal that he is, Tom is identified just enough with "proper" society to wish not to be publicly seen with the "juvenile pariah of the village." Tom's idea turns out to have promise, and, with Huck's input, it turns into a strategy for finding and claiming the treasure.

Chapter XXVIII

Armed with a stash of stolen keys, Tom and Huck wait outside the tavern until it is safe to use one of the keys to get inside the room hiding the treasure. "Meowing" like a cat is one of their secret signals. The boys eventually make their move, but in vain. After Tom comes upon Joe—immobilized on the floor and half conscious from alcohol consumption—he nearly steps on the villain's hand, and both boys are seized by enough "terror and excitement" to "burst" their hearts. The plan is postponed to another night.

Chapter XXIX

In this chapter, two plot lines are developed simultaneously. Social outcast Huck Finn stays vigilantly on the clandestine treasure hunt, while Tom goes aboard a ferry with Becky and the rest of the "giddy and rollicking company" to the Thatcher family's elaborate picnic downriver. Tom breaks the rules before the ferry has even left the landing: With little resistance, he persuades Becky to disobey her mother's orders about where to stay for the night with promises of ice cream with the widow Douglas and other adventures. After "[all] the different ways of getting hot and tired were gone through with" at the picnic site, the two head off for McDougal's formidable cave.

Twain's description of the cave is written exactly as it would be remembered from childhood experiences. The cave is dangerous and deliriously exciting—a labyrinth of chasms, rifts, and canyonlike "avenues." To a child's imagination, it suggests—beyond grand adventuring—darkness, danger, and the ever-present fear of being lost and abandoned.

As the happy and exhausted picnickers are making their return on the ferry, Huck is still standing vigil over the tavern site, waiting to be called upon for some kind of exciting action. The sudden sight of two men scurrying in the darkness is Huck's summons. One is carrying a box Huck takes to be the treasure, and Huck follows undetected. They arrive at the widow Douglas's house, where Huck overhears another dreadful conversation—a second act of revenge plotted by Injun Joe, this time against the widow because of an earlier act of her husband's, and this time in a manner more fitting a horror movie than a child's adventure story. Hearing Joe's plan to disfigure the woman's face jolts Huck out of his paralyzing fear, and, his good nature aroused, he runs—not directly to the rescue—but for help. Despite having a name unlikely "to open many doors," Huck manages to get the Welchman to open his, and he and his sons race to help widow Douglas, their neighbor. His good deed accomplished, Huck races in the opposite direction.

Chapter XXX

For a brief time, Huck is accorded a well-deserved place at the center of the action. His effort to save the widow Douglas was successful, and the town at large is now in pursuit of Joe disguised as a whiskered Spaniard and his "ragged" accomplice. When the kindly Welchman coaxes from reluctant Huck the revelation of the Spaniard's true identity, he makes the disturbing assumption that "Injuns" like Joe are capable of particularly vicious acts that no white man would commit: "notching ears and slitting noses . . . white men don't take that sort of revenge. But an Injun! That's a different matter altogether."

This comment about Injun Joe is a notable example of Twain's prejudicial view of Native Americans—a bias he finally seemed to surmount, but not as authentically or generously as he did the other manifestations of racism of his time, especially against blacks. A wealth of critical commentary has been produced on this issue. (See especially Carter Revard's essay, "Why Mark Twain Murdered Injun Joe—And Will Never be Indicted" in the Norton Critical Edition of *Tom Sawyer*, pp. 332–52.)

In conversation with the Welchman, Huck nearly reveals his knowledge of the treasure but hastily suggests instead that the villains' recovered bundle contained Sunday school books—a notion so implausible as to set the Welchman laughing. Huck then realizes that the existence of the treasure is still not widely known, leaving Tom and him to claim it for themselves. Huck has another moment of vicarious success, recognition, and glory when the widow Douglas arrives with townspeople and is told that her life was saved by a yet-to-be-identified person.

The discovery that Tom and Becky are missing occurs in church the next day in a scene reminiscent of a parent's nightmare. The collective conclusion is that they are still in the cave, lost, and perhaps dead. The scene that follows, in which the entire town is instantly focused on rescuing their lost children, provides a comforting respite for readers who have endured the frightful scenes with Injun Joe. "The alarm swept from lip to lip, from group to group, from street to street, and within five minutes the bells were wildly clanging and the whole town was up!" For "three dreadful days and nights" the search dragged on, exhausting everyone until the town "sank into a hopeless stupor."

Meanwhile Huck, fallen ill and not told about Tom and Becky's disappearance, is being cared for by widow Douglas. In the coming together of the widow and child, Twain gives expression to a folksy affirmation of democracy:

> Whether [Huck] was good, bad, or indifferent, [she] would do her best by him, because . . . he was the Lord's, and nothing that was the Lord's was a thing to be neglected. . . . The Lord [puts his mark] somewhere on every creature that comes from his hands.

Chapter XXXI

This chapter returns the reader to dark and mysterious places. In a tone both high-spirited and menacing, it recounts Tom and Becky's exploration of the wonders of the cave: spacious caverns, a bewitching spring, a subterranean lake, stalactites and stalagmites, natural staircases, old signatures etched with candle smoke onto the walls, and little knots of bats, then swarms of them, that chase the children deeper into the shadows. Tom and Becky are lost in their adventuring and then more seriously lost in what Becky calls a "mixed-up crooked-ness." In the face of their duress, Tom keeps up his spirits, but he is not heroic or even very resourceful and Becky devolves into whimpering passivity. Gamely, she finally concedes that it is as much her fault they are lost as it is his.

Just when it seems conditions could not get worse—their candles and food are gone and they are nearly delirious with hunger and fatigue—Tom suddenly catches sight of Injun Joe's light and then of Injun Joe himself, also hiding in the cave.

Chapter XXXII

On Tuesday night—after three days of searching—Mrs. Thatcher was roused from her delirium, Aunt Polly from her "settled melancholy," and the town from its "sad and forlorn" rest by the sounds of bells ringing and cries of "They're found! They're found!" Tom had discovered a tiny aperture in the earthen wall out of which he saw the Mississippi River flowing by, 5 miles from their point of entrance. Both are rescued and fall temporarily ill from their ordeal. After recovering, Tom meets up with Huck to exchange the details of their separate adventures, and Tom gets the news—intended to be comforting but shocking instead—that Judge Thatcher has inadvertently sealed off the cave entrance with Injun Joe inside.

Chapter XXXIII

The news of Joe's entrapment brings out the townspeople again—motivated more by macabre curiosity than concern. Once exposed, the details of Joe's grisly death by starvation become clear. Tom is briefly moved to feel sympathy because of his own recent experience of entrapment but then is more sensibly moved by relief that Joe is no longer a danger to him or Huck. Joe's funeral—a well-attended public event—resembles a picnic in mood and is said to have been as satisfactory as a hanging. The exact object of Twain's satire here is again left for the reader to ponder. Inexplicably, some townspeople are disappointed to have missed out on rallying around a public petition calling for clemency for Joe. Perhaps Twain is satirizing people's desire for melodrama, the more improbable the cause, the more satisfying.

Huck and Tom then conspire to make more plans. Huck is elated to learn the treasure is not lost, as he had imagined, and off they go in a "borrowed" skiff back to Tom's secret entrance to the cave. After announcing that from now on they will be known as Tom's Gang and plotting their future career as mere robbers and ransom raisers (because robbing, unlike pirating, can be done "close to home and circuses and all that"), the boys head into the cave. Speculation about the whereabouts and intentions of Joe's ghost dampens the boys's excitement, but only briefly. The treasure is finally found along with guns and other paraphernalia suitable for their future in crime.

On their way home, with all plans for dividing and hiding the money agreed upon, Huck and Tom are waylaid by the Welchman, who leads them to the widow Douglas's house for an undisclosed celebration. With reluctance (more from Huck, less from Tom) each boy must shed his clothes, stained with candle grease and clay, and get "slicked up" in a fancy donated suit.

Chapter XXXIV

The sight of fancy clothes and a group of dressed-up townspeople makes Huck want to jump out a window, but Tom is willing to go through with the event. Huck is soon identified by the Welchman as the real hero of the widow's rescue. Huck's "reward"—announced by the grateful widow with great fanfare and good intentions—could scarcely be less pleasing to Huck. He is to be properly housed, dressed, and educated. Now it is Tom's turn to rescue Huck. He announces that Huck needs no such special attentions because he is rich. To the skeptical onlookers, Tom produces the bagful of gold coins. "The spectacle took the general breath away."

Chapter XXXV

Now in possession of such an unimaginable sum of money, Tom and Huck assume celebrity status in town; this new elevation prevents them from enjoying their old "ordinary" lives: no commonplace speech or aimless wandering about. Judge Thatcher and the widow Douglas—the respectable adults—take on the task of managing the boys' wealth, arranging that each earn as interest a sum greater than the minister's annual salary. The town seems to be carried away with vicarious enjoyment of the boys' good fortune; Judge Thatcher, for example, upon learning from Becky that Tom lied to take her punishment, declares it a "noble, generous, and magnanimous" lie, "worthy . . . to march down through history breast to breast with George Washington's lauded Truth about the hatchet!"

All things considered, the boys' good fortune yields some unpleasant realities, especially for Huck, who is "intolerably uncomfortable" with all his new comforts. Especially unfortunate, according to the narrator, is that Huck's acquiring of "proper" speech has rendered his conversations "insipid." He endures these miseries for three weeks and then disappears. Tom knows where to find him and does—"unkempt, uncombed . . . clad in the same ruin of rags . . ." and content once again. Tom, the surprisingly conventional one, urges conformity—*"Everybody does that way, Huck"*—but Huck, the incorrigible "outsider" and true rebel, has the last word: "I ain't everybody, and I can't *stand* it." (It is Huck who will become Mark Twain's most compelling and complex protagonist in his own series of adventures.)

Tom's descent into ordinariness and Huck's self-elevation from uncomfortable comfort and dull respectability form the novel's conclusion, but the narrator does not give up on keeping these two bright spirits aligned. Eventually, they will part company, but for now, Huck is willing to give respectability another try for the chance to be a robber in Tom Sawyer's gang.

Conclusion

This story, insists the narrator, must come to a close because it has promised to be about boys and these boys are too soon to become men. Sometime later, we have reason to hope, we, the readers, will find out what happened to this generation of St. Petersburg citizens.

Critical Views

HENRY NASH SMITH ON
TOM SAWYER, INADEQUATE HERO

The images of Tom in church or Tom whooping and prancing along the sand bar remain in the reader's mind after Mark Twain's struggles with plot and subplot and point of view are forgotten. They belong to his primary alphabet of symbols. Their importance for his subsequent career requires us to examine them with care.

Tom is a kind of embryonic Everyman. In church and school he confronts institutions that seem to him alien and at times hostile; on Jackson's Island he enjoys comradeship with his fellows and he responds to the physical environment. Natural man beleaguered by society, but able to gain happiness by escaping to the forest and the river: this is undoubtedly an important aspect of the meaning that thousands of readers have found in the novel. In situations of this sort nineteenth-century writers were likely to be led by the heritage of Romantic thought to identify themselves with the virtuous hero and to ascribe evil exclusively to society. The signs of such a tendency on the part of Mark Twain himself can be discerned in *Tom Sawyer*. But the church and the school are not truly evil, they are merely inconvenient and tedious; Tom doesn't really intend running away for good; his playing pirate is a child's fantasy, and can with perfect appropriateness have its climax in the boys' return:

> Suddenly the minister shouted at the top of his voice: "Praise God from whom all blessings flow—SING! and put your hearts in it!"
> And they did. Old Hundred swelled up with a triumphant burst, and while it shook the rafters Tom Sawyer the Pirate looked around upon the envying juveniles about him and confessed in his heart that this was the proudest moment of his life.

As the "sold" congregation trooped out they said they would almost be willing to be made ridiculous again to hear Old Hundred sung like that once more.

Here Tom is fully integrated with the community (which is identical with the congregation in the church); the community is completely harmonious within itself; and the general exultation finds expression in the singing of a Christian hymn at the command of the minister. The official culture of St. Petersburg could hardly receive a more absolute affirmation.

It is the absence of a basic conflict between Tom and the society of the village that obliges Mark Twain to look elsewhere for the conflict he considered essential to the plot of a novel. He solves his problem by introducing evil in the form of Injun Joe, whose mixed blood labels him an outsider. Tom and Huck fear him, and Tom is sufficiently aggressive to testify against him in court, but a direct collision is out of the question and Injun Joe has to be destroyed unintentionally by Judge Thatcher when he seals up the mouth of the cave.

While acknowledging, at least tacitly, the artificiality of this subplot, Bernard DeVoto emphasized its importance in contributing to *Tom Sawyer* "murder and starvation, grave-robbery and revenge, terror and panic, some of the darkest emotions of men, some of the most terrible fears of children." He believed such materials were an important aspect of the book's fidelity to human experience. It is an idyll, he pointed out, but it is enclosed in dread; and this keeps it true to the world of boyhood. The argument has weight. Yet a melodramatic villain tends to evoke a melodramatic hero, and Mark Twain does not entirely resist the temptation. He evades the naive moral categories of the Sunday-school books by making Tom a boy who is "bad" according to their standards yet "good" according to more profound criteria. The demonstration, however, is not enough to give Tom real depth of character. The reader is evidently meant to see Tom's badness as nothing more than endearing mischief, indicative of a normal amount of imagination and energy; it is not bad at all. Mark Twain has written the Sunday-school story about the Good Little Boy Who Succeeded all over again with only a slight change in the hero's make-up and costume.

If the Matter of Hannibal is to be explored by means of a plot involving a protagonist of this sort, two basic situations are possible. We may have the naturally good hero enjoying a triumphant and harmonious relation with his society (Tom in church while the Doxology is being sung), or the naturally good hero at odds with his society (Tom suffering during the minister's prayer). The first of these alternatives could yield nothing except an endorsement of conventional values. The second alternative was more promising; it at least offered a built-in conflict and a point of view adapted to satire of existing institutions. But *Tom Sawyer* shows how dangerous the idea of the hero's natural goodness was as literary material. It constantly threatened to become merely a stereotype because of the difficulty of imagining a kind of goodness basically different from that endorsed by the accepted value system. Francis Parkman, for example, wishing to praise his French-Canadian guide across the plains, Henry Chatillon, said he had a "natural refinement."

Mark Twain would ultimately need a hero more hostile toward the dominant culture than Tom Sawyer was—Tom, the devotee of the "rules," the exponent of doing things by the book, the respectable boy who took out his impulses toward rebellion in harmless fantasies of escape. It is appropriate that *The Adventures of Tom Sawyer* ends with Tom made wealthy by the treasure he has found, acclaimed as a hero, and basking in the approval of both his sweetheart and her father. His last act is to persuade Huck to return to the Widow Douglas' and be "respectable." No doubt this wind-up of the plot was dictated by "the exigencies of romantic literature" which Mark Twain later said accounted for the death of Injun Joe in the cave. In the brief conclusion he almost explicitly confesses that the conventions of the novel as he has adopted them in *Tom Sawyer* have proved to be poorly suited to his materials.

This perception was probably aided by the fact that even before he had finished the book he had recognized the solution for several of his technical problems. It lay in using Huck Finn as a narrative persona. The outcast Huck was far more alienated than Tom from conventional values. Telling a story in Huck's words would allow Mark Twain to exploit fully the color of vernacular speech. At the same time, the use of a narrator who was also a principal actor in the story would virtually compel the writer to maintain a consistent point of view.

In a fashion that recalls Cooper's discovery of unexpected possibilities in Leatherstocking while he was writing *The Pioneers*, Mark Twain seems to grow suddenly aware of Huck's potential importance only a few pages before the end of *Tom Sawyer*. Huck performs his first significant act in Chapter 29 by giving the alarm to Mr. Jones and his sons, who frustrate Injun Joe's plot against the Widow Douglas. The conversation between Huck and the Joneses is reported at surprising length. Mark Twain has evidently become interested both in the workings of Huck's mind and in his speech; he exhibits him in the process of inventing a cover story—an activity that would become almost compulsive in *Adventures of Huckleberry Finn*. Huck's impulse to run away when he learns that the townspeople have gathered to honor him and Tom in a great civic ceremony and his sufferings under the regimen imposed on him by the well-intentioned Widow Douglas are not merely prophetic of the sequel, they merge imperceptibly with the opening chapters that Mark Twain would begin to write as soon as he had finished *Tom Sawyer*. Indeed, Tom figures too prominently for the taste of most readers in both the opening and the closing chapters of the later novel. But the differences between the two books—aptly illustrated by the contrast between the tone of the chapters of *Huckleberry Finn* in which Tom appears and the tone of those in which he does not— greatly outweigh the similarities. *Tom Sawyer* provides relatively little opportunity to deal with the problem of values to which Mark Twain had devoted so much attention in his early work; *Huckleberry Finn* is his major effort in this direction.

The adults [in *Tom Sawyer*] are engaged in showing off as much as are the children. If Tom apes the authorities of romance, Mr. Walters, the Sunday school superintendent, has his own authorities which he likewise strives to emulate:

> This superintendent was a slim creature of thirty-five, with a sandy goatee and short sandy hair; he wore a stiff standing-collar whose upper edge almost reached his ears and whose sharp points curved forward abreast the corners of his mouth—a fence that compelled a straight lookout ahead, and a turning of the whole body when a side view was required; his chin was propped on a spreading cravat which was as broad and as long as a bank-note, and had fringed ends; his boot-toes were turned sharply up, in the fashion of the day, like sleigh-runners— an effect patiently and laboriously produced by the young men by sitting with their toes pressed against a wall for hours together. Mr. Walters was very earnest of mien, and very sincere and honest at heart; and he held sacred things and places in such reverence, and so separated them from worldly matters, that unconsciously to himself his Sunday-school voice had acquired a peculiar intonation which was wholly absent on week-days.[14]

Mr. Walters, like Tom, puts on style. Indeed, the whole village, adults as well as children, puts on style of various sorts on various occasions—all for the purpose of showing off. On the opening page of the book, Aunt Polly has to look for Tom over the top of her spectacles because "they were her state pair, the pride of her heart, and were built for 'style,' not service—she could have seen through a pair of stove-lids just as well." The style of *Tom Sawyer* is the vision which at once looks over and exposes the old dead styles which are impersonated and gently burlesqued as the boy stages his action.

If Tom must stage his shows, he is doing no more than the adults who are busily engaged in staging their own performances, casting the children as characters. At the end of the Sunday school episode, for example, as the Thatchers make their impressive entrance, Tom occupies himself by showing off for Becky and the rest of the society shows off for the impressive Judge Thatcher.

> Mr. Walters fell to "showing off," with all sorts of official bustlings and activities, giving orders, delivering judgments, discharging directions here, there, everywhere that he could find a target. The librarian "showed off"—running hither and thither with his arms full of books and making a deal of the splutter and fuss that insect authority delights in. The young lady teachers "showed off"—bending sweetly over pupils that were lately being boxed, lifting pretty warning fingers at bad little boys and patting good ones lovingly. The young gentlemen teachers "showed off" with small scoldings and other little displays of authority and fine attention to discipline. . . . The little girls "showed off" in various ways and the little boys "showed off" with such diligence that the air was thick with paper wads and the murmur of scufflings. And above it all the great man sat and beamed a majestic judicial smile upon all the house, and warmed himself in the sun of his own grandeur—for he was "showing off," too.[15]

The satiric direction of this passage points to the activity which unites the entire community, from the revered judge down to the youngest child. The entire Sunday school is a show in which everyone is showing off. No sooner are the Thatchers seated than Mr. Walters proceeds to the next act of his performance—the delivery of the Bible prize to the student who had earned the most tickets for memorizing Bible verses. This little act gives him a chance—the language of the book unfailingly discloses the terms of the action—to "exhibit a prodigy." Tom, however, steals the scene. Having traded spoils taken at the whitewashing exploit for tickets awarded to Bible quoters, he emerges with the largest number of tickets, to the amazement and envy of the little showmen he has outmaneuvered. His performance elevates him to the height of Judge Thatcher. "It was the most stunning surprise of the decade, and so profound was the sensation that it lifted the new hero up to the judicial one's altitude, and the school had two marvels to gaze upon in place of one."[16]

The Sunday school is merely one of the shows in St. Petersburg. The sermon which follows is another. While the minister drearily enacts his performance, Tom, again cast into the background, becomes interested only upon hearing the minister say that at the millennium when the lion and lamb should lie down together a little child should lead the world's hosts. This is the minister's verbal effort to produce a great scene. "But the pathos, the lesson, the moral of the great spectacle were lost upon the boy; he only thought of the conspicuousness of the principal character before the onlooking nations; his face lit with the thought, and he said to himself that he wished he could be that child, if it was a tame lion."[17] Unable to effect such a miracle, Tom does the next best thing, which is to set up a competing act. Releasing a pinch bug, he succeeds in diverting attention from the minister and—when a dog chances to sit upon the beetle—breaking up the minister's performance completely. . . .

What every episode of *Tom Sawyer* enacts is the conversion of all "serious" community activity—all duty, pain, grief, and work—into pleasure and play. Tom Sawyer himself is the agent of this conversion. His imaginative force, his *reality*, lies precisely in his capacity to make his dreams and fantasies come "true" in the form of "acts" which entertain the villagers. Nowhere is David Riesman's fine observation, that glamour in an actor measures the apathy in the audience, better borne out than in the world of *Tom Sawyer*.[19] For Tom's glittering power, his heroism, invariably defines at the same time it feeds upon the boredom of the villagers.

In discovering Tom, Mark Twain had actually gained a new perspective on himself as entertainer, for he had managed to objectify in a new character the possibilities of the pleasure principle. The method of objectification was the burlesque-indulgent perspective upon the world of boyhood. Such a perspective enabled Mark Twain to see, in a way no writer had seen before him, an entire area of action where entertainment dissolved into play. In seeing it he recognized possibilities of both entertainment and play which he himself could have but dimly imagined prior to the emergence of *Tom Sawyer*.

For the real audacity of *Tom Sawyer* is its commitment to the pleasure principle. Though the book participates in parody, burlesque, and satire, it clearly cannot be characterized by any of these terms. It is, after all, a tale—an *adventure*—and its commitment is not to exposing sham, as in the case of satire; nor is it to mocking a prior art form as in the case of parody and burlesque. Instead, the positive force—the force to which the world of St. Petersburg succumbs—is play itself.

Play is the reality principle in the book. What makes Tom Sawyer seem more real than the adults who submit to his power is his capacity to take his pleasure openly in the form of make-believe while they take theirs covertly under the guise of seriousness. Tom's virtue lies not in his good heart, his independence, or his pluck—none of which he really has—but in his truth to the pleasure principle which is the ultimate reality of the enchanted idyll. The very enchantment results from the indulgent perspective the author assumes toward the action. The narrator's indulgence is none other than the pleasure he takes in disclosing the play world.

The coupling of the outer pleasure with the inner world of play causes Tom's make-believe to seem true, whereas the adult "reality" and "duty" appear false and pretentious. This conversion, not so much process as point of view, is at once the humor and truth of the book. By inventing Tom Sawyer, Mark Twain had actually succeeded in dramatizing in a fictional narrative the possibilities of entertainment. He had projected through Tom Sawyer's imagination a world of boyhood in which play was the central reality, the defining value. The money Tom discovers in the cave in the final episode is a reward not for his courage or heroism—the indulgent perspective discloses his cowardice and essential self-love—but for his capacity to have dreamed it into reality with his make-believe imagination. And Tom quite characteristically appears before the townspeople to show off his treasure in one last exhibitionistic fling before the final curtain. The world of boyhood as it emerges in the pages of *Tom Sawyer* is a world where play, make-believe, and adventure are the living realities defining the false pieties and platitudes which constitute the dull pleasure of the adult world.

Mark Twain's invention of Tom Sawyer and his invention of the novel are thus one and the same thing. The reality principle of this first independent fiction is, as we have seen, play. The approach to fiction through the boy-character of a master player is an index to Mark Twain's inability to "believe" in conventional fiction. The exaggerated contempt in which he held fiction was his characteristic "humor" embodying his true perception. Mark Twain had no real use for conventional fiction because his entire genius——the "Mark Twain" in Samuel Clemens—had his being in the tall tale, a form which presented the truth as a lie, whereas the fiction he condemned presented the lie as the truth. That is why Mark Twain could say to Howells that he would not take Tom Sawyer into manhood because he "would just be like all the other one horse men in literature." Though he had promised in his conclusion to trace his figures into adult life, he never did; he could only call the changeless Tom Sawyer back on stage for more—and poorer—"acts."

In moving to the form of fiction, Mark Twain subverted the conventions of the form, not only by means of the burlesque and indulgent perspectives, but also through the character of Tom himself, whose "adventure" or plot is projected in terms of play and make-believe. The enchantment, the idyll, and the boy—the chief components of the book—create fiction as play instead of as truth. The book is no testimonial to the child's unfettered imagination transcending the materialism of the adult world. Instead, it creates existence under the name of pleasure, and portrays all human actions, no matter how "serious," as forms of play. Thus the imagination is shorn of the religious, romantic, and transcendental meanings with which Coleridge invested it; in Mark Twain's world of boyhood, the imagination represents the capacity for mimicry, impersonation, make-believe, and play. That is why the boy of Mark Twain's idyll is so different from the child of Wordsworth's vision. The child of the romantic poet has a direct relationship to God and Nature. Mark Twain's boy has a direct relationship to pleasure. The romantic child *is*, has being; Mark Twain's boy plays, has pleasure.

Notes

14. *Writings*, XII, pp. 35–36.
15. *Ibid.*, p. 38.
16. *Ibid.*, p. 39.
17. *Ibid.*, p. 47.
19. David Riesman, *The Lonely Crowd* (New Haven, 1950), p. 313.

JUDITH FETTERLEY ON TOM AS A LOCAL ANTIDOTE TO BOREDOM

One of the major rhythms of *The Adventures of Tom Sawyer* is established in its opening lines: "'Tom!' No answer. 'Tom!' No answer. 'What's gone with that boy, I wonder? You, TOM!'"[1] Much of the action of the novel is a variation on this theme of looking for Tom, for in the world of St. Petersburg the boy, Tom, is central. It is he who creates the major occasions for the town, and the emotional arcs of the book are described by his being lost or found. When Tom is thought lost, the town is in dismay; when he is found, it rejoices:

The alarm swept from lip to lip, from group to group, from street to street, and within five minutes the bells were wildly clanging and the whole town was up! The Cardiff Hill episode sank into instant insignificance, the burglars were forgotten, horses were saddled, skiffs were manned, the ferryboat ordered out, and before the horror was half an hour old two hundred men were pouring down highroad and river toward the cave (p. 248).

Away in the middle of the night a wild peal burst from the village bells and in a moment the streets were swarming with frantic half-clad people, who shouted, "Turn out! turn out! they're found! they're found!" Tin pans and horns were added to the din, the population massed itself and moved toward the river, met the children coming in an open carriage drawn by shouting citizens, thronged around it, joined its homeward march, and swept magnificently up the main street roaring huzzah after huzzah! (pp. 263–64).

The world of St. Petersburg is dull and sleepy, and its arch enemy is the boredom which lies at its heart, making it so sensation-hungry that everything that happens is greeted as an entertainment. Thus the discovery of Dr. Robinson's murder constitutes a local holiday for which school is dismissed. Thus the town turns out to fill the church as never before for the spectacle of a triple funeral. Thus the trial of Muff Potter is the biggest entertainment of the summer, and when Tom finally decides to testify at the trial, he does so as much out of a sense of what is dramatically appropriate and will improve the show as he does out of a tormented conscience.

The boredom which lies at the heart of St. Petersburg is most fully pictured in the scenes which take place in the Sunday school and church the first Sunday of the novel. The dreadful monotony of Sunday school text, of prayer and sermon, the painful rigidity of never-varying rituals, symbolized by the superintendent's clothes—"a fence that compelled a straight lookout ahead, and a turning of the whole body when a side view was required" (p. 35)—is relieved only by a few paper wads, an occasional scuffle, a fly to be caught. The world of St. Petersburg is trapped into boredom by its own hypocrisy, by its refusal to admit how dull and uninteresting the things which it professes to value really are. It is against this background that Tom's centrality to St. Petersburg can be understood. He provides life, interest, amusement; he is a master entertainer with a bug for every occasion. No wonder St. Petersburg is always looking for Tom.

One of the central scenes which defines this aspect of the interrelation of Tom and his society is the moment in church when Tom discovers and releases his pinch bug. Tom's boredom has reached painful proportions; the momentary flicker of interest aroused by the image of the little child leading the lion and lamb before the hosts at Judgment Day has faded. Then he remembers his pinch bug, a "treasure" of the first order. He takes it out, it bites him, and he flips it on the floor. Immediately the congregation stirs itself; at last something is happening. A few minutes later a poodle which is the very image of the congregation, bored and sleepy, comes along and, like the congregation, begins to take an interest in the bug and to play with it. But after awhile he forgets about the bug and in starting to go to sleep, sits on it, whereupon it promptly bites him and sends him tearing around the church and ultimately out a window. "Tom Sawyer went home quite cheerful, thinking to himself that there was some satisfaction about divine service when there was a bit of variety in it" (p. 49). He has provided a brilliant entertainment and won the thanks of the congregation, for his act has not only amused them but has made it impossible for church to continue.

The other center of boredom in this world is school, and once again Tom has a bug to relieve him. Tom is bored to a point almost beyond endurance when he sticks his hand in his pocket and discovers the tick he has just purchased from Huck Finn: "his face lit up with a glow of gratitude that was prayer" (p. 65). His comrade, Joe Harper, as painfully bored as Tom, greets the tick and its promise of pleasure "deeply and grate-fully" (p. 66). The language which describes the discovery of the tick is an impressive index of the boredom of school. But again the boys are not the only ones bored. The schoolmaster, Mr. Dobbins, is asleep when Tom comes in and only wakes up long enough to switch him. Tom's tick and his play with it become equally the source of the schoolmaster's interest: "He had contemplated a good part of the performance before he contributed his bit of variety to it" (p. 67). The switching is part of the complex game which the boys and adults play in order to make school bearable. It is the mode by which the teacher is allowed to save face and keep on professing his interest in school. It in no way prevents Tom from continuing to create interest through his pranks, for, unlike the world of Dickens, the switching in Tom's world leaves neither psychological nor physical scars. It is, indeed, the mark of the boys' success in gaining attention and creating interest; it is a modest form of showing off for both boys and teacher. The relationship between the adults and children in this novel is deeply symbiotic.

Tom's interactions with Aunt Polly develop another dimension of this relationship. Aunt Polly, like the rest of St. Petersburg, loves Tom, because he makes her laugh and gives variety to her life. But Aunt Polly expresses her affection for Tom by constantly rapping him on the head with her thimble, setting traps to catch him in lies, carping at him for being bad and breaking her heart, and enforcing labor on his holidays. She never comes out and openly says what Tom means to her until she thinks he is dead. In part, Aunt Polly is a victim of her own hypocrisy and unreality. She refuses to take account of the split which she everywhere expresses between her heart and her conscience, with its conception of duty. Thus she is never free to say what she truly feels. But this is really a very small part of the psychology behind Aunt Polly's actions. Tom knows that Aunt Polly's thimble on his head, like Dobbins's switching, is an index of the place he holds in her heart; thus he worries only when she does not rap him. But much more important, Tom knows that it is her resistance, her posture of disapproval, which creates his pleasure.

The fact that the boys' world of pranks is no fun without the existence of an adult world to prohibit them is made clear in a number of scenes in the story. When school is finally over and vacation finally comes, there is nothing Tom wants to do. What has happened to the lure of Cardiff Hill, which called to him so irresistibly through the schoolroom window? Clearly "hooky" is one thing and vacation another. When the boys run off to Jackson's Island everything is bully for the first day or so, but pretty soon they lose interest in going naked and sleeping out in the open and swimming whenever they want, because, as Joe says, "Swimming's no good. I don't seem to care for it, somehow, when there ain't anybody to say I shan't go in" (p. 138). But perhaps the most famous instance of this principle is the whitewashing episode, which casts Tom in the role of discovering it as a great law of human nature. The success of Tom's strategy rests on his intuitive discovery that people want to do what they are forbidden to. In order to change white-washing from hard labor into the one thing the boys are mad to do Tom has only to present it as something he cannot allow them to do, an art requiring special skill which only he pos-sesses, a task which he is under strict orders to perform only himself without help from anyone else. By means of this tactic Tom not only gets the boys to do the whitewashing for him; he gets them to pay him for the privilege.

The Adventures of Tom Sawyer is steeped in the rhythm of this relationship between adults and children. The delight of midnight trips is in creeping out of the window in answer to a secret signal and in defiance of an adult stricture. The pleasure of Huck Finn's society, like the attractiveness of his state, lies in its being forbidden. When Huck first enters the book, it is this angle from which he is viewed. Thus he is described as a "romantic outcast," a phrase which defines the point of view on him as Tom's. There is at this point no hint of what Huck's life might be like either from his point of view or the narrator's. The strong implication, however, is that the joys of his existence are imaginary, a product of prohibition. Huck is introduced in the book in great part as an element in Mark Twain's creation of the dynamic between pleasure and prohibition in the mind of Tom Sawyer. And Mark Twain's achievement in creating this dynamic in *The Adventures of Tom Sawyer* prepares us for Tom's passion for creating obstacles at the end of *Huckleberry Finn*. It is part and parcel of his conception of pleasure. If the adults have failed to fulfill their part of the game and provide difficulties for Tom to overcome, then he will simply have to play both parts and create the obstacles himself. That a new mode of pleasure has been discovered to the reader in the process of Huck's adventures is not Tom's fault; he is doing only what he thinks is expected of him.

Note
    1. Samuel L. Clemens, *The Adventures of Tom Sawyer* in *The Writings of Mark Twain*, Definitive Edition (New York: Gabriel Wells, 1922–25), VIII, 1. Subsequent references will be to this edition of *Tom Sawyer* and will be included in parentheses in the text.

LEE CLARK MITCHELL ON APPEARANCE AND VOICE IN THE NOVEL

Given the intense focus of everyone else's attention on Tom Sawyer, it may come as something of a shock to realize how little he is actually seen or shown, how minimally in fact the novel ever describes or specifically places him. Consider how few questions can be answered about his past (when and how was he orphaned? why is Sid his half-brother?), or even how little we know of his actual physique. Numerous illustrators have created for us the image of a barefoot boy, but no confirmation exists in the novel that he ever dons a tattered straw hat, or sports a chequered shirt, or that his overalls are either ragged or barely held up by suspenders. We cannot even be altogether certain of his age. And that may be part of the novel's point: Tom's very emptiness as a physical signifier encourages readers to project their separate ideas and fantasies, to fill in the faceless shape that Mark Twain so vaguely delineates.[13] If so, the irony of the novel is twofold: that despite its silence, early illustrators imposed an image of Tom on the text that remains for most readers vivid enough to make them forget it is not in the text; and yet, that within the novel, Tom's elaborate dramas of 'showing off' curiously avail him nothing in terms of either physical or visual description.

    Nor are other characters described with any greater precision, reducing the entire village of St Petersburg to shadowy gestures and physical types, some signalled only through the most fleeting of metonymic identifications. Aunt Polly is simply identified as a pair of spectacles 'built for "style"' (p. 9), while the new boy in town is likewise equated with the natty jacket, bright necktie, dainty cap, shining shoes, and 'citified air' he wears (p. 13). While the Widow Douglas appears as merely 'fair, smart, and forty', Jim, 'the small coloured boy', is granted no description at all (pp. 42, 11). Becky Thatcher is portrayed more completely than any other child, and yet the terms are so stereotypical as to make her seem not more, but less distinctive: 'a lovely little blue-eyed creature with yellow hair plaited into two long tails, white summer frock, and embroidered pantalettes' (p. 26). Joe Harper, Amy Lawrence, Huck Finn, and the other children, like Injun Joe, Muff Potter, Judge Thatcher, and most of the other adults are all equally undefined. Indeed, the novel offers only a single exception to this descriptive rule, in the painfully ample depiction of Mr Walters, the school superintendent:

> This superintendent was a slim creature of thirty-five, with a sandy goatee, and short sandy hair; he wore a stiff standing-collar whose upper edge almost reached his ears, and whose sharp points curved forward abreast the corners of his mouth—a fence that compelled a straight look-out ahead, and a turning of the whole body when a side view was required. His chin was propped on a spreading cravat, which was as broad and as long as a bank-note, and had fringed ends, his boot toes were turned sharply up, in the fashion of the day, like sleighrunners—an effect patiently and laboriously produced by the young men by sitting with their toes pressed against a wall for hours together. Mr. Walters was very earnest of mien, and very sincere and honest at heart. (p. 36).

It is as if a full physical description were to be invoked only in order to diminish a person, making him vivid as a corporeal presence because so insignificant otherwise.

Supporting this argument is the extremely thin portrait offered of Injun Joe, who serves as something like a grim reality principle for the novel. He too is never described, even though Tom and Huck repeatedly freeze in fear at the sudden sight of his 'stolid face' (p. 89). Within the idyllic world that Mark Twain conjures up as St Petersburg, 'iron faced' Injun Joe represents the existence of unadulterated evil and death, the necessary 'Et in Arcadia Ego' to this pastoral on the Mississippi (p. 167). And if, in a peculiar fashion, he seems to compete with Tom for the town's undivided attention, the difference between the two is imaged in the differences between their two deaths: Tom's repeated false alarms and the fraud of his elaborately staged funeral versus Injun Joe's excruciating experience of burial alive, slowly starved to death on a diet of old candles and raw bats, like something out of Edgar Allan Poe. 'Injun Joe is Tom's shadow self,' Cynthia Griffin Wolff has observed, and his presence in the novel is 'as if one element in Tom's fantasy world has torn loose and broken away from him, roaming restlessly—a ruthless predator—genuinely and mortally dangerous'.[14] What makes Injun Joe's presence all the more menacing, of course, is that that presence is no more detailed than Tom's, his psychological 'shadow self'.

Even so, the remarkable feature of Injun Joe's appearance lies less in the vagueness of his physical characteristics than in the frequency with which he is signalled in the novel by sound alone. Tom first recognizes this menacing Other only when he begins to speak: 'Say, Huck, I know another o' them voices; it's Injun Joe' (p. 76). And when the villain is later significantly disguised as a 'deaf and dumb Spaniard', it is his unexpected, angry outburst that betrays him: 'This voice made the boys gasp and quake. It was Injun Joe's!' (p. 182). Indeed, many of the novel's characters are denoted by their distinctive voices—from Aunt Polly's opening, stentorian 'Tom' to Huck Finn's closingly ebullient, 'Now, that's something *like*' (p. 245). And the reason that Tom Sawyer seems to us the most vivid character of all is that his personality is conveyed so fully in a characteristic manner of speech. Despite his vague physical features, we hear him come fully alive through the charm of his speech.

Notes

13. As James M. Cox has observed: 'it is impossible to tell what he looks like—how tall, how heavy, how handsome or ugly he is. He emerges as the figure, the *character*, of the Boy.' See *The Fate of Humor*, 133–4.

14. Cynthia Griffin Wolff, '*The Adventures of Tom Sawyer*: A Nightmare Vision of American Boyhood', *Massachusetts Review*, 21 (Winter 1980), 647–8.

E.L. DOCTOROW ON THE CHILD READER AND THE ADULT READER

Ever since its publication in 1876, children have been able to read *Tom Sawyer* with a sense of recognition for the feelings of childhood truly rendered: how Tom finds solace for his unjust treatment at the hands of Aunt Polly by dreaming of running away; or how he loves Becky Thatcher, the sort of simpering little blond girl all boys love, and how he does the absolutely right thing in lying and taking her punishment in school to protect her; or how he and his friends pretend to be pirates or the Merry Men of Sherwood Forest, accurately interrupting their scenarios with arguments about who plays what part and what everyone must say and how they must fight and when they must die. In addition, child readers recognize as true and reasonable Tom's aversion to soap and water; they share his keen interest in the insect forms of life, and they relish the not always kind attention he pays to dogs and cats. They understand the value he and his friends place on such items as pulled teeth, marbles, tadpoles, pieces of colored glass. And because all children are given to myth and superstition, they take as seriously as he does the proper rituals and necessary incantations for ridding oneself of warts or reclaiming lost possessions by using the divining powers of doodlebugs, as well as the efficacy of various spells, charms, and oaths drawn in blood, although it is sadly possible that children today, divested of their atavistic impulses by television cartoons and computer games, are no longer the natural repositories of such folklore. . . .

The moral failures of the adult culture of St. Petersburgh are apparent to the child reader. They range from the imperceptions of the dithering Aunt Polly to the pure evil of Injun Joe. When, with chapter 9, the plot of the book is finally engaged, that is, when Tom and Huckleberry Finn witness the murder at night in the graveyard, the young reader finds everything from then on seriously satisfying, as how could it not be, in that it involves the fear of a murderer, the terror of being lost in a cave, the gratification of a court trial that rights an injustice, and the apotheosis of Tom Sawyer as hero of the whole town and possessor of a vast fortune.

Even more satisfying, though not to be consciously admitted as such, is the uniting of the child and adult communities in times of crisis. The whole town turns out along the river when it appears that Tom and Joe Harper have drowned. There is universal mourning. Similarly, when Tom and Becky are feared lost in the cave, the bereavement is understood as the entire community's. The government of the adults is washed away in their tearful expressions of love. And the young reader confirms his own hope that no matter how troubled his relations with his elders may be, beneath all their disapproval is their underlying love for him, constant and steadfast. This is the ultimate subtextual assurance Mark Twain provides his young reader, and it is no small thing for the child who understands, at whatever degree of consciousness, that his own transgressions are never as dire as they seem, and that there is a bond that unites old and young in one moral world in which truth can be realized and forgiveness is always possible.

But what the adult eye reads—ah, that is quite another matter. We open the book now and see Tom as a mysterious fellow, possibly, something of an anthropological construct, more a pastiche of boyhood qualities than a boy. He is a collection of traits we recognize as applicable to boyhood, or to American boyhood, all of them brought together and animated by the author's voice. In their encyclopedic accuracy they confer upon Tom an unnatural vividness rather than a human character. . . .

Unlike Lewis Carroll's Alice, Tom does not have to drink anything to grow taller or shorter. (I note that the illustrations to the first edition can't seem to decide on Tom's proper height or bulk or the lineaments of his face.) He's a morally plastic trickster in part derived from the Trickster myths of the Afro-American and Native American traditions. He may also be the flighty, whimsical, sometimes kind, sometimes cruel minor sort of deity of classical myth, a god of mischief, with the capacity to manipulate the actions of normal human beings, evoke and deflect human emotions, and in general to arrange the course of history to bring honor to himself.

We do not minimize Mark Twain's achievement by noticing, as adults, some of the means by which it was accomplished. Tom Sawyer's thought has generative powers. What he fantasizes often comes to pass. In chapter 3 he receives a cuffing from his aunt when it is the detestable Sid who has broken the sugar bowl; in the sulking aftermath, he pictures himself "brought home from the river, dead, with his curls all wet and his sore heart at rest. How she [Aunt Polly] would throw herself upon him, and how her tears would fall like rain, and her lips pray God to give her back her boy and she would never, never abuse him any more! But he would lie there . . . and make no sign." As indeed he doesn't in chapter 15 when he hides under Aunt Polly's bed, still wet from his night swim, and listens as she weeps and mourns just as he once imagined, and remonstrates with herself in the belief that he has drowned. Tom's fantasies of buried pirate treasure metamorphose into the real buried treasure of Injun Joe. And after Tom and Huck thrill themselves imagining the devilish goings-on in grave-yards at midnight in chapter 6, real deviltry arises in front of their eyes in chapter 9, when the grave robbers appear and fight among themselves until one of them is murdered in cold blood. Possibly we are ourselves witness to the author's explor-atory method of composition, in which he first conceives of likely things for a boy's mind to imagine, and then decides some of them are too good not to be developed and played out as elements of a plot.

Albert E. Stone Offers Some General Remarks

No American author has participated more fully in his or her country's life, during a crucial era of change, than Samuel L. Clemens. Merely to summarize the signal features of the life of the man known as Mark Twain authenticates this claim. Consider this incomplete review of personal and cultural events and aspects: childhood in a Mississippi River border town of the slaveholding South; piloting and journeyman printing along the great Midwestern river; brief Civil War service in the Confederate militia; westward adventuring along the Oregon Trail to the Nevada silver mines and California gold mines; newspaper reporting and humorous lecturing on the Pacific Slope and Hawaii; an eastward voyage via the Isthmus to New York City and a wider, more successful career as reporter, freelance writer, and lyceum lecturer; national and European travel by rail and steamboat, culminating in an around-the-world tour; marriage into the Eastern monied class and residence in Hartford's Nook Farm neighborhood of genteel writers and liberal clergymen; authorship of a succession of popular travel books and novels marketed by subscription; his own publishing company as one of several speculations, ending in the 1890s in bankruptcy.

In the course of this archetypal Gilded Age history Mark Twain also shared the political, social, and intellectual concerns of his contemporaries. Some of these were liberal Republican politics during and after Reconstruction; Darwinism, determininism, and the Social Gospel; new psychological models of the mind; comprehensive disillusionment later, and bitter criticism of imperialism and racism in the wake of the Spanish-American War and Jim Crow. As reflections of his age, his books sometimes became plays on the New York stage; even more of them were translated into foreign languages, winning him worldwide acclaim. At the zenith of his remarkable (and sometimes tragic and tormented) career, the white-haired, white-suited Mark Twain modestly acknowledged what had already been said of him—this flamboyant American had become the most widely known literary figure on the planet.

At the center of this fabulous private and public life stand Mark Twain's twin monuments of fiction, *The Adventures of Tom Sawyer* and *Adventures of Huckleberry Finn*. In these two novels, one published in 1876, the other in 1885, live a pair of immortal boys. Tom Sawyer and Huck Finn are among America's undisputed contributions to the world's cast of unforgettable characters. As Bernard DeVoto put it, "these two boys have become the possessions of everyone. . . . they have become legends."[1] . . .

Doubtless the deepest and most fertile tension in Mark Twain's consciousness was his lifelong dedication to his boyhood experiences and outlook as these came into conflict with adult values and compromises. His ambivalence about and celebration of boyhood opened the richest vein in his art, impelling him to juxtapose the innocent, passive eye of childhood against mature wisdom, hypocrisy, and evil. . . . Twain and his contemporaries shared an intense nostalgia for childhood, the small town, and an antebellum America apparently light-years away from the often bleak and brutal conditions of their own day.

The Adventures of Tom Sawyer in particular epitomizes this cultural convergence. For *Tom Sawyer* was but one of a series of postwar novels celebrating boyhood by presenting the Bad Boy as a distinctively new American hero of fiction. . . .

Because its author tried to make *Tom Sawyer* part of this juvenile culture—"my book is intended mainly for the entertainment of boys and girls," runs the final preface—there is a close link between this Bad Boy and his literary cousins. Comparing Tom with his fellow anti-prigs displays striking parallels and differences. First of all, Tom is no stereotype of the Bad Boy, the Natural Boy, the Human Boy. He is himself, an individual with distinctive traits, speech, social personality. Further, the ties connecting him to St. Petersburgh* are more complex and deep-rooted than is true of the other village boys. In spite of a veneer of farcical humor, Tom's adventures, unlike those of his fellows, become the serious process by which this boy matures. As a result, *Tom Sawyer* is more than a nostalgic re-creation of Mississippi River life before the war, though it is that, too. Twain pays boyhood a greater compliment by making his Tom the vehicle of a full-dress study of personal identity in social terms at once genial and searching. . . .

[The] author of *Tom Sawyer* and *Huckleberry Finn* (if not of *Pudd'nhead Wilson*) was a prude. As writer, he was hypersensitive to his readers and his own timidities. Consequently, as a motive for human conduct in growing boys and girls, adolescents, or adults, sexuality is almost entirely absent from his fiction. Even in unpublished writings he exhibited unusual reticence. "There was the utmost liberty among young people—," he wrote, recalling Hannibal in the sketch "Villagers of 1840–3," "but no young girl was ever insulted, or seduced, or even scandalously gossiped about. Such things were not even dreamed of in that society, much less spoken of and referred to as possibilities."[17]

Twain, in common with his contemporaries (even Stephen Crane), shied away from the fact of sexuality in curious young minds, not only because of convention but also out of deep-seated ambivalence in respect to time and change. Sexuality inevitably implied adolescence, growth toward adulthood. With part of his mind he turned his back on such implications, taking pains never to specify Tom's age. From the first, Tom and Huck were conceived as children of indefinite years. Presexual innocence absolved Twain from confronting certain aspects of maturity, especially physical love and marriage, which neither his abilities nor his predilections equipped him to develop satisfactorily. Boyhood, about which no one of his generation wrote better, was a safer, more congenial area of personal and social experience. There he could focus on timeless moments in late childhood or early adolescence in which a boy, poised between infancy and manhood, could face forward to certain grown-up problems—serious ones, too, like money and death, though not, in this book, slavery—and yet backward to a state before puberty. *Tom Sawyer's* conclusion puts as explicitly as Twain was able this precarious position. "So endeth this chronicle. It being strictly a history of a boy, it must stop here; the story could not go much further without becoming the history of a *man*. When one writes a novel about grown people, he knows exactly where to stop— that is, with a marriage; but when he writes of juveniles, he must stop where he best can" (275).

Tom Sawyer is punctuated with moments embodying this quality of arrested time. Several take place on Cardiff Hill, that "Delectable Land, dreamy, reposeful, and inviting" (26). Others show Tom squirming at his school desk. The two sites are symbolic. One is natural and static, the other social and on the move. As unwilling schoolboy, Tom "ached to be free, or else to have something of interest to do to pass the dreary time" (72–73). Here Tom shows his double-mindedness, to face both ways, whether to escape back into time by doing something actively exciting, or to escape to the timeless woods and river. Thus the plot is constructed so that Tom's escape adventures are keyed to the temporal fife of the larger community. In a way quite unlike Aldrich, Warner, Howe, or Howells, Twain has his boy predict or repeat in the boy world occurrences in the grown-up world. On the night after Tom and Joe Harper pretend to kill each other in the Robin Hood game, Tom witnesses the actual murder of Dr. Robinson. Similarly, Tom and Becky on a picnic narrowly escape from the same cave where Injun Joe meets a grim death. Readers can readily recall other parallels or anticipations.

The link between the two worlds is invariably Tom Sawyer. Joe Harper plays Robin Hood, and Huck watches the graveyard murder, but only Tom does both. Participating in this way means that Tom gradually experiences the cruelties, cupidities, greed, and responsibilities of adulthood. This maturation is the dramatic and satiric undercurrent during the early part of the book but becomes the major motif as his extended summer wears to a climax. In the process, St. Petersburgh assumes a larger role than do the locales of the other village Bad Boy stories. The town in *Tom Sawyer* emerges as more than the setting of a golden idyll; it sits for its portrait (one of the first in our literature) as a representative American community. People of all classes and castes inhabit Twain's town—lawyers and drunkards, white boys and girls, mulattoes and a young slave named Jim, schoolmasters and old maids and Indian half-breeds. Something suggesting the total social reality of a typical antebellum river town is sketched. . . .

If Mark Twain did become disenchanted with Tom Sawyer—after all, one image of Sam Clemens himself—then the boy's easy acceptance of village respectability remains in striking contrast with another side of boyhood exemplified by Huck Finn. Passive acquiescence to a beautifully corrupted community vitiates for many modern readers the flair, independence, and moral sensitivity Tom shows at key points earlier in the narrative. In a deep sense, Tom Sawyer has gone over to the real enemy—time. For his initiation, by turns admirable and incomplete, goes a long way toward bringing him out of the eternal moment of boyhood, symbolized by Cardiff Hill, and launching him on the stream of social time or history. The aging writer may have confirmed this disguised but disillusioning outcome for his character when he derisively termed Theodore Roosevelt the political Tom Sawyer of the Spanish-American War era.[23]

On all counts, Twain's initial exploration in fiction of his own childhood turned up no permanent Paradise by the river. "Those good old simple days" that he and his fellow Americans yearned for held a full measure of personal and social evil. This historical insight was perhaps not suitable (or even interesting) to good little girls and boys. But it was a perception and prophecy Mark Twain could not fully hide from himself. If *Tom Sawyer* began as a prose hymn to the personal and national past, it ended as also a deceptively detached study of a soiled society, one both static and changing. Like the Natural Boy himself, life and art proved a mixture of good and evil, of play and horror. This powerfully simple insight into a cultural moment and monument accounts for much of the book's century-long appeal and present significance.

Notes

* I have retained the spelling "St. Petersburgh" with the "h" because it is that of the first American edition reproduced here, although it appears as "St. Petersburg" without the "h" in subsequent editions.

1. Bernard DeVoto, *Mark Twain's America* (Boston: Little Brown, 1932), 299–300.

17. Quoted in Dixon Wecter, *Sam Clemens of Hannibal* (Boston: Houghton Mifflin, 1952), 173.

23. Justin Kaplan, *Mr. Clemens and Mark Twain* (New York: Simon and Schuster, 1966), 363.

MICHAEL J. KISKIS RECONSIDERS TWAIN'S VALUES

In December 1909, Mark Twain penned what he called "the final chapter of my autobiography." The essay, published posthumously in 1911 as "The Death of Jean," has received only quick mention by biographers and has been passed off as highly sentimentalized, yet it is one of the more affective pieces in Twain's canon (frankly, I have found no piece so likely to destroy conventional notions of Mark Twain). Critics have been content to slip the piece among those works considered extraordinary not because it hints at a genuine domestic foundation in Twain's emotional life (though this is a valuable and neglected aspect of Twain's life and writing) but because it does not conform to established, comfortable ideas of Twain as misanthropic social philosopher. It challenges the established paradigm and is, therefore, relegated to the ash heap of sentimentalism. Mark Twain, it seems, is not allowed to express real and troubling emotion. And we, as critics, are made uncomfortable by that emotion and must look away before we admit that Twain had (and maybe that we have) an emotional life.

Some biographical background may be helpful here. In the summer of 1909, Jean Clemens, Twain's youngest daughter, arrived in Redding, Connecticut, to rejoin the Clemens household (to reconstitute that household may be a more accurate description since Clara would marry in October and later move to Europe). The aging Twain, who by this time had watched the procession of the dead as a genuinely interested bystander, was pleased with the potential for reconnecting with Jean, who had been shuttled back and forth between a maze of sanitoriums and cures since her diagnosis with epilepsy in the 1890s. Their relationship had been a difficult one. And while all Twain's relationships were difficult, none bore so tragic a tint as those with his children.

With a potential reconciliation in sight, Jean dies on the morning of Christmas Eve. She seems to have suffered a seizure and drowned in her bath. She is found by the household's servant, Katy Leary. Twain begins:

> Jean is dead!
>
> Has anyone ever tried to put upon paper all the little happenings connected with a dear one—happenings of the twenty-four hours preceding the sudden and unexpected death of that dear one? Would a book contain them? Would two books contain them? I think not. They pour into the mind in a flood. They are little things that have been always happening every day, and were always so unimportant and easily forgettable before—but now! Now, how different! how precious they are, how dear, how unforgettable, how pathetic, how sacred, how clothed with dignity! (*AU*, 245–46)

Twain's calm is extremely affective here. Throughout his career he was haunted by a tendency to burlesque and melodramatic pathos at moments of personal stress; however, here there are no histrionics, no melodramatic expression of grief. The grief is there. And it is deep. But it is present not in the specific experience of Jean's death but in the catalog of deaths that Twain creates as he replays his past:

> In England thirteen years ago, my wife and I were stabbed to the heart with a cablegram which said, "Susy was mercifully released today." I had to send a like shock to Clara, in Berlin, this morning. . . .

I lost Susy thirteen years ago; I lost her mother—her incomparable mother!—five and a half years ago; Clara has gone away to life in Europe; and now I have lost Jean. How poor I am, who was once so rich!

... Twain finally faces the image of his own death as he transports himself to the site of Jean's arrival and burial in Elmira. He did not make the funeral journey, but he imagines the scene:

2:30 P.M.—It is the time appointed. The funeral has begun. Four hundred miles away, but I can see it all, just as if I were there. The scene is the library, in the Langdon homestead. Jean's coffin stands where her mother and I stood, forty years ago, and were married; and where Susy's coffin stood thirteen years ago; where her mother's stood, five years and a half ago; and where mine will stand, after a little time. (*AU*, 252)

The deadpan voice that Twain used so expertly in his humor is here translated into a mechanism to relate emotional fullness and the exhaustion that is companion to grief. There is resignation and, as he has said earlier, contentment in the realization of his coming participation in the family pageant. Bitterness, anger, frustration have been put aside so that he can focus on reclaiming family attachment. Four months later Twain died of congestive heart failure. His coffin did stand in that same room.

But how does this evaluation of Twain's emotional tie to family enter into the established critical tradition within Twain studies? It doesn't. At this point, Twain is, by most accounts, bitter, cynical, railing against God and the universe, and taking every opportunity available to hoot and toss epithets at the possibility of human redemption. Critics, biographers, and scholars have taken an odd form (a perverse form?) of delight in perpetuating this sour image of Mark Twain. Yes, his comments carried strong indictments of human foolishness and folly. Yes, he saw the worst in humans, and especially saw the worst in himself. But there is much more to Twain than that, and this is not particularly good news to those still embedded in the Brooks-DeVoto argument or those who insist on Twain's exclusive title as definer of American individualism. . . .

I am arguing for a more complex reading of Mark Twain's work and an acknowledgment of and an appreciation for his connection to literary domesticity. Tom Sawyer, Huck Finn, Hank Morgan, Joan of Arc, Roxy, and Adam and Eve: all suffer the most domestic of ills—the inability to negotiate human relationships. And no matter how we turn away from this to find more seductive, more broadly political, more socially sophisticated readings, we still must face the reality at the heart of Twain's stories—that pain is at the center of home and grows out of the search for home.

At the end of *The Adventures of Tom Sawyer*, Twain offers an exchange between Huck and Tom that epitomizes that pain. Huck is considering escape from his newly assigned place in the home of Widow Douglas. Tom, however, will have none of that:

> " . . . Huck, we can't let you in the gang if you ain't respectable, you know."
> Huck's joy was quenched.
> "Can't let me in, Tom? Didn't you let me go for a pirate?"
> "Yes, but that's different. A robber is more high-toned than what a pirate is—as a general thing. In most countries they're awful high up in the nobility—dukes and such."
> "Now Tom, hain't you always been friendly to me? You wouldn't shet me out, would you, Tom? You wouldn't do that, now, would you, Tom?"
> "Huck, I wouldn't want to, and I don't want to—but what would people say? Why they'd say, 'Mph! Tom Sawyer's Gang! pretty low characters in it!' *They'd mean you, Huck*. You wouldn't like that, and I wouldn't."[5]

Of course, Huck caves in to this pressure. Despite Tom's condescension, despite what we might, I think rightly, interpret as

Tom's deep ambivalence (I am tempted to say hatred) toward the desperate boy, Huck gives in. He needs to belong. To someone. To something. And so does Twain. Once more to the end of "The Death of Jean":

> It is all over.
> When Clara went away two weeks ago to live in Europe, it was hard, but I could bear it, for I had Jean left. I said we would be a family. We said we would be close comrades and happy—just we two. That fair dream was in my mind when Jean met me at the steamer last Monday; it was in my mind when she received me at the door last Tuesday evening. We were together; we were a family! The dream had come true—oh, preciously true, contentedly true, satisfyingly true! and remained true two whole days.
> And now? Now Jean is in her grave!
> In the grave—if I can believe it. God rest her sweet spirit! (*AU, 252*)

Ultimately, Twain's work recounts the struggle of the human heart to find a place in this world, to find peace, to find a place to lie comfortably content with our mortality. To find a home. To hear the whine of the spinning wheel and think not of the mournfulest sound but of the peace of your own bed.

Mark Twain eventually left behind the hoax, joke, and tall tale for the more powerful images of community and home. In fact, he sought out the dilemmas of personal relationships as the basis for his storytelling. Whereas power, the lust for it and the failure to achieve it, is a focal point in many of Mark Twain's tales, he is at his best in those pieces that focus on domestic relationships: the childhood bluster at the opening to *The Adventures of Tom Sawyer*; the raft episodes in *Adventures of Huckleberry Finn*; the memories of an old and disappointed lover in *Personal Recollections of Joan of Arc*; the domestic fiction in the McWilliams short stories, the animal tales, the stories of the good and bad boys; and the anecdotes that creep into his speeches and his autobiography. This argues for complexity; however, we often continue to focus on "The Notorious Jumping Frog of Calaveras County," "Grandfather's Old Ram," "Dick Baker's Cat," along with a host of tales that fit our expectation of Twain's frontier roots, even those in *Innocents Abroad*. . . .

Twain scholars would now do well to see that the humor of the old Southwest is only one of the influences and, perhaps, not a dominant influence after all. The frontier boast was an effective tool for Twain. But he had a good deal more success when he set aside the wool and furs of the frontier for the homespun and silk of the household.

Note

5. Twain, *Adventures of Tom Sawyer*, 235. Hereafter referred to as *ATS*.

JOHN BIRD EXAMINES TWAIN'S DOUBLE NARRATOR STRATEGY

[Critic] William M. Gibson maintains, "[W]henever the narrator [in *Tom Sawyer*] spoke to the adult reader about his young characters he tended to weaken these parts of the book; whereas in the strong episodes he presented the boys' actions—both overt and psychological—dramatically, without editorial comment." In a recent study, Peter Messent blames the lack of unity on the "omniscient and retrospective narration," asserting that "Twain's use of satire, burlesque and sentimentality often run in uneasy relationship to one another."[15]

Indeed, the narrator is conventional and stilted, and perhaps even worse, at times stuffy, clichéd, and trite. And as Messent points out, the shifts between satire and sentimentality are often abrupt and hard to reconcile. We can blame these problems on various things: Twain's relative inexperience with extended fiction—this was, as Gibson notes, only his second. . . .

[The] problems with the narrator of *Tom Sawyer* raise a number of questions. How could Mark Twain, at the height of his powers, create such a narrator, one so full of cliché and conventionality? More to the point, why would he, when in other works of the same period he was able to create narrators with fresh, vital vision? If the narrator is so problematic, how did the novel rise above its continuously weak narrative presence to achieve its status as, to quote Gerber again, "a book one never forgets" (*TS*, xiv)?

I propose that the answer to these questions may lie in our close identification of the narrator with the author, an identification fueled by the text, but one that I believe is at least partly erroneous. In this stilted and conventional narrator, Mark Twain created a character distinct from himself, distinct from his usual persona, and a character that, I will argue, we are *supposed* to find stilted and trite. Further, I propose that there is not just one narrator of *Tom Sawyer*, but two: this stilted, conventional narrator and the fresher, more lively narrator . . . in the scenes that shift closer to Tom's point of view. I suggest that we can best see this distance and distinctness by examining both narrators' language, specifically their metaphorical language. Because metaphor is so fundamental to both a writer's linguistic characteristics and his personal vision, it can function as a kind of linguistic fingerprint. If we look at each narrator's metaphorical language, comparing it to that in other writings from the period that plainly do have Mark Twain as narrator, we will see a definite distinction. We can most clearly see the way the narrator becomes more lively when his point of view nears Tom's in the way his metaphors shift from clichéd and dead to fresh and alive. In other words, this shift is not merely one from literary language to vernacular language, as Gerber sees it; rather, it is a shift in metaphorical vision. Because these shifts are so carefully controlled, the narrative point of view works consistently on a double level. Thus, this seemingly flawed narrator is actually two separate narrators, and rather than constituting a flaw, this narrative split actually contributes to the depth and success of the novel. Further, the narrative split not only explains the confusion often felt by an earlier generation of largely formalist critics, but also answers the serious charges of more recent cultural critics concerning the novel's putative moral blindness.[17]

We can get a clear sense of what I am calling the "conventional narrator" by quoting any of the idyllic set pieces that open many chapters. The first paragraph of chapter 2, the introduction to the whitewashing scene, shows this narrator very well: "Saturday morning was come, and all the summer world was bright and fresh, and brimming with life. There was a song in every heart; and if the heart was young the music issued at the lips. There was cheer in every face and a spring in every step. The locust trees were in bloom and the fragrance of the blossoms filled the air. Cardiff Hill, beyond the village and above it, was green with vegetation, and it lay just far enough away to see a Delectable Land, dreamy, reposeful, and inviting" (*TS*, 10). Part of the effect of this paragraph comes, I think, from the preponderance of dead metaphor, so dead it is worse than cliché: "the summer world was bright and fresh, and brimming with life"; "a song in every heart"; "cheer in every face and a spring in every step." The one original metaphor, comparing Cardiff Hill to "a Delectable Land," complete with capital letters, is so stilted and literary that it loses any intended metaphorical flavor. . . .

This narrator can string together dead metaphor at will: "These despised themselves, as being the dupes of a wily fraud, a guileful snake in the grass" (*TS*, 34); "Tom was introduced to the judge; but his tongue was tied, his breath would hardly come, his heart quaked" (*TS*, 35); "how her tears would fall like rain" (*TS*, 22); "would she heave one little sigh to see a bright young life so rudely blighted, so untimely cut down?" (*TS*, 25).

Yet the novel also contains metaphorical language that is lively and inventive, revealing a vernacular vision and attitude rather than the conventional literary vision typified by the clichés just quoted. For example, here is the description of Tom after his Sunday morning bath: "But when he emerged from the towel, he was not yet satisfactory; for the clean territory stopped short at his chin and jaws, like a mask; below and beyond this line there was a dark expanse of unirrigated soil that spread downward in front and backward around his neck" (*TS*, 28). . . .

How can one novel contain such conflicting metaphorical visions? Is this a sign of Twain's inexperience as a fiction writer, or an indication of his conflicted mental state, or his inability to write in a sustained vernacular style? I don't think it's any of these things, and we have already seen ample proof of his skill in his works up to this time, particularly in "Old Times on the Mississippi," which he wrote at about the same time as *Tom Sawyer*. . . .

Why could he not do so in *Tom Sawyer*? I propose that he could, but chose not to, that the conventional narrator of parts of *Tom Sawyer* is not the familiar persona Mark Twain, but another persona, one that we are supposed to recognize and reject. There are *two* narrators here, the novel is richer for it, and we can see that only by examining metaphorical language.

At the end of the whitewashing incident, the narrator interrupts the scene to tell us that Tom "had discovered a great law of human action, without knowing it" (*TS*, 16). Henry Nash Smith notes, "The incident is reduced to an exemplum illustrating a generalization that has nothing to do with the story." Smith sees this as a result of the "burlesque interpos[ing] a considerable psychological distance between himself and his characters," but I would argue instead that Twain is giving us a clear signal about the identity of the narrator and, more importantly, how we are supposed to respond to his dead vision. The key language is this: "If he [Tom] had been a great and wise philosopher, like the writer of this book, he would have comprehended . . ." (*TS*, 16). Smith comments, "Something tells the writer he is on the wrong tack and he confuses things further by mocking at himself," but I propose that Twain is satirizing here the very notion of "The Author." We are to take the phrase "great and wise philosopher" not as Twain's mocking himself, but as Twain's mocking writers who see themselves as "great and wise philosophers," who see themselves as "Author," which is the name I give to this narrator with the dead metaphorical vision.[18]

An extended sequence in the Examination Evening scene offers further and more substantial proof of the existence of two narrators. After all the recitations, "the prime feature of the evening" is "original 'compositions' by the young ladies" (*TS*, 156). The narrative voice is the lively narrator, the satiric Mark Twain we are used to from works such as *Life on the Mississippi*, especially the parts that follow what was originally "Old Times." The narrator tells us:

> A prevalent feature in these compositions was a nursed and petted melancholy; another was a wasteful and opulent gush of "fine language;" another was a tendency to lug in by the ears particularly prized words and phrases until they were worn entirely out; and a peculiarity that conspicuously marked and marred them was the inveterate and intolerable sermon that wagged its crippled tail at the end of each and every one of them. No matter what the subject might be, a brainracking effort was made to squirm it into some aspect or other that the moral and religious mind could contemplate with edification. (*TS*, 156)

Then we get several examples of these "prize authors":

> The first composition that was read was one entitled "Is this, then, Life?" Perhaps the reader can endure an extract from it:

> > "In the common walks of life, with what delightful emotions does the youthful mind look forward to some anticipated scene of festivity! Imagination is busy sketching rose-tinted pictures of joy. In fancy, the voluptuous votary of fashion sees herself amid the festive throng, the observed of all observers. Her graceful form, arrayed in snowy robes, is whirling through the mazes of the joyous dance; her eye is brightest, her step is lightest in the gay assembly." (*TS*, 156–57)

This narrator may as well be describing and lampooning the narrator I am calling "Author." The last composition, "A Vision," concludes with this immortal simile: "A strange sadness rested upon her features, like icy tears upon the robe of December, as she pointed to the contending elements without, and bade me contemplate the two beings presented" (*TS*, 159). As the narrator comments, "This nightmare occupied some ten pages of manuscript and wound up with a sermon so destructive of all hope to non-Presbyterians that it took the first prize" (*TS*, 159).

Rather than being an anomaly in the text, this lampooning of overwrought literary language has actually been going on throughout, as the two narrative visions have been conflicting with one another. In a typical chapter in the first half of the novel, "Author" begins; then the narrator with the fresher metaphorical vision takes over; then the scene shifts totally to dialogue and action. At the end of a typical chapter, "Author" is apt to return and make a comment. In the scenes where the language becomes most overwrought, as in the scenes where Tom mopes around wishing for death because Becky Thatcher has rejected him, the lively narrator emerges and dashes dirty washwater on the prostrate Tom, metaphorically splashing "Author" back to reality. . . .

"Author" reemerges much later in the novel, when Injun Joe's corpse is found. The description of how "the poor unfortunate had starved to death" is deliciously purple:

The captive had broken off the stalagmite, and upon the stump had placed a stone wherein he had scooped a shallow hollow to catch the precious drop that fell once in every three minutes with the dreary regularity of a clock-tick—a dessert spoonful once in four and twenty hours. That drop was falling when the Pyramids were new; when Troy fell; when the foundations of Rome were laid; when Christ was crucified; when the Conqueror created the British empire; when Columbus sailed; when the massacre at Lexington was "news." It is falling now; it will still be falling when all these things shall have sunk down the afternoon of history, and the twilight of tradition, and been swallowed up in the thick night of oblivion. (*TS*, 239–40)

"Author" goes on to draw a message from this sermon, making his "composition" worthy of a first prize on Examination Evening. Henry Nash Smith misreads the passage, I think; he argues that "such a burst of eloquence is quite out of keeping with the tone of the book. It serves no purpose except to demonstrate that the narrator can produce the kind of associations held in esteem by the dominant culture."[20] I see the language as perfectly in keeping with the tone of the book, at least the part of the tone that is set by "Author," and as serving the purpose not of pleasing the dominant culture, but of showing the dominant culture the hollowness and deadness of its prized language. . . .

I began this section by quoting Twain's letter to Howells about perhaps making a mistake in not choosing a first-person narrator for his boy book. We know what astonishing results came when he did choose to do so, and what a world of trouble he raised by finding that remarkable voice and style. What we have not fully seen yet is how crucial metaphor is to voice and style, and even more deeply, to vision and theme. Metaphor carries us to the heart of the novel that is the heart of Mark Twain's career.

Notes

15. John C. Gerber, "*Adventures of Tom Sawyer, The*," 14; Gibson, *Art of Mark Twain*, 99; Messent, *Mark Twain*, 67–68.

17. Gerber, "*Adventures of Tom Sawyer*," 14. Wonham has already noted a narrative split. In *Mark Twain and the Art of the Tall Tale*, 128–32, he adroitly outlines what he calls a contest for narrative authority between the narrator and Tom Sawyer, with Tom serving as the tall-tale narrator who subverts the main narrator's conventional values. Wonham's point is persuasive and powerful, but I am arguing that the narrative contest is even more complex.

18. Smith, *Mark Twain*, 83. The narrator I am calling "Author" could also be an example of what Michelson calls a "Petrified Man." Michelson, *Mark Twain on the Loose*, 14–18.

20. Smith, *Mark Twain*, 84.

The sections of *The Adventures of Tom Sawyer* covering church life, despite a clearly satirical tone, contain as well sentimental details, such as the moment when the sermon reaches its climax: "[Tom] was really interested for a little while. The minister made a grand and moving picture of the assembling together of the world's hosts at the millennium when the lion and the lamb should lie down together and a little child should lead them."[16] While it is true that Twain does immediately deflate this transcendent vision by explaining Tom's inability to grasp it, the sheer wonder represented is a telling detail.

On the other hand, he certainly did recognize the negative legacy of his religious upbringing. Still some critics have been far too negative in their portrayals of Hannibal's harmful effects upon young Sam. The chief example of this is the very early depiction by Van Wyck Brooks, who perpetrated numerous distortions regarding Hannibal and his mother's religious influence: the town was a "desert of human sand!—the barrenest spot in all Christendom, surely, for the seed of genius to fall in. . . . [frontier Missouri] was not happy: it was a dark jumble of decayed faiths, of unconfessed class distinctions, of inarticulate misery. . . . It was a horde-life, a herd-life, an epoch without sun or stars, the twilight of a human spirit."[17] As Ron Powers has remarked, "Seldom has a recognized scholar been more drastically self-deluded, and with more destructive consequences, about the crucial resonance between an artist and the artist's formative habitat."[18]

Still we must concede that in Twain's mind, there were negative aspects to small-town life in Hannibal. Twain's Sunday school or church passages in *Tom Sawyer*, *The Gilded Age*, *Adventures of Huckleberry Finn*, and elsewhere are notable for their oppressive and enervating tone. Certainly Twain often poked fun at the silliness of the churches of his youth. In *Tom Sawyer* the key features of church life appear to be "showing off" and brainless conformity, such as in the story of the boy who "once recited three thousand verses [of Scripture] without stopping; but the strain upon his mental faculties was too great, and he was little better than an idiot from that day forth."[19] This comic episode suggests (and criticizes) the way religious language is consumed by the general populace: memorization without meaning or reflection that precludes any in-depth examination of the religious texts themselves. In many ways, the idiot child of Twain's anecdote is representative of all the evolving (or devolving) generations who consume the language without reflection and are won over by the art and in turn have forsaken the underlying reality (attitudes memorably captured in the posthumously published essay "Corn-Pone Opinions"). Later Tom is able to trade a variety of materials for the colored tokens in order to be presented with the prize Bible before the learned and honored guests by Judge Temple, who takes the opportunity to wax eloquent about this fine young Christian boy: "it's all owing to right bringing up."[20] Similarly, in *The Gilded Age*, the corrupt Senator Dilsworthy addresses a Sunday school with reverence and pious charm, ending by claiming that "All that he is, he owes to Sunday-school."[21] The irony of the speech consists of the allusion to the Sunday school as source of "all that he is"—meaning, hypocrisy, hidden corruption, and the ability to manipulate institutional religion to foster docility and conformity.

These examples and many more underscore a religious skepticism that attacks the prevailing myth of the small town and the Sunday schools—a myth of which Twain became profoundly aware at an early age. The small town, with the church and its Sunday school squarely at its center, became reified in the minds of many Americans as abstract symbol of all things good, pure, and right about their society. The mythic concept of the town was attacked by a number of savage critics of middle-class American civilization who reached an apogee of influence just after World War I in the movement known as the "revolt from the village," led by the likes of Sherwood Anderson and Sinclair Lewis. But this revolt began much earlier, in the antebellum period with the masters of Southwestern humor, and reignited just after the Civil War ended and the Gilded Age commenced.

In Edward Eggleston's *The Hoosier Schoolmaster* (1871), for example, one long and memorable chapter entitled "The Hardshell Preacher" pokes good fun at the small-town church run by the "Hardshell" type of minister: "prodigiously illiterate, and often vicious. Some of their preachers are notorious drunkards."[22] Besides the sheer delight created by Eggleston's remarkable ear for dialect, this chapter is easily compared with similar sections in *Tom Sawyer* and *Huckleberry Finn*: the interminable, drowsy sermon; Tom playing with a pinch-bug (in Eggleston's book, a green lizard); and the satirical references to old-time revivalism when the King in *Huckleberry Finn* becomes a revivalist at a camp meeting associated in antebellum times with such groups as the "New York Perfectionists," the "Millerites," and the "Campbellites." Twain often poked fun at this sort of revivalism, as in the brief autobiographical note recorded in his youth: "Campbellite revival. All converted but me. All sinners again in a week."[23]

Notes
16. *The Adventures of Tom Sawyer*, 68.
17. Brooks quoted in Powers, *Dangerous Water*, 57.
18. Powers, *Dangerous Water*, 57.
19. *The Adventures of Tom Sawyer*, 60.
20. Ibid., 64.
21. *The Gilded Age*, 481–82.
22. Edward Eggleston, *The Hoosier Schoolmaster*, 102.
23. Quoted in Wecter, *Sam Clemens of Hannibal*, 88.

ROY BLOUNT, JR. ON TWAIN AS POLITICAL COMMENTATOR

What, if anything, about this benighted moment of American life will anyone in the future look back on with nostalgia? Well, those of us who have cable are experiencing a golden age of sarcasm (from the Greek *sarkazein*, "to chew the lips in rage"). Jon Stewart, Stephen Colbert, Bill Maher and Keith Olbermann are digging into our direst forebodings so adroitly and intensely that we may want to cry, "Stop tickling!" Forget earnest punditry. In a world of hollow White House pronouncements, evaporating mainstream media and metastasizing bloggery, it's the mocking heads who make something like sense.

Let not those heads swell, however. News in the form of edgy drollery may seem a brave new thing, but it can all be traced back to one source, the man Ernest Hemingway said all of modern American literature could be traced back to: Mark Twain. Oh, that old cracker-barrel guy, you may say. White suit, cigar, reports of my death have been greatly exaggerated—but he died back in 1910, no? White, male, and didn't he write in dialect? What does he have to do with the issues of our day?

As it happens, many of these were also the issues of his day, and he addressed them as eloquently as anyone has since. The idea that America is a Christian nation? Andrew Carnegie brought that up to him once. "Why, Carnegie," Twain answered, "so is Hell."

What about those Abu Ghraib photographs? In "King Leopold's Soliloquy," a fulminating essay he published in 1905, when he was a very cantankerous 70, Twain imagines the ruler of Belgium pitying himself for the inconvenience of photos showing natives of the Congo whose hands have been cut off by Belgian exploiters. In the good old days, Leopold complains, he could deny atrocities and be believed. "Then all of a sudden came the crash! That is to say, the incorruptible Kodak—and all the harmony went to hell! The only witness I have encountered in my long experience that I couldn't bribe."

Waterboarding? In 1902, American soldiers were involved in a war to suppress rebels in the Philippines, which the U.S. had taken from Spain in the Spanish-American War, then decided to keep for itself instead of granting the Filipinos the independence they thought they had been promised. That outcome enraged Twain. So did "the torturing of Filipinos by the awful 'water-cure.'"

"To make them confess—what?" Twain asked. "Truth? Or lies? How can one know which it is they are telling? For under unendurable pain a man confesses anything that is required of him, true or false, and his evidence is worthless."

Whether Twain was talking about racism at home, the foreign misadventures of the Western powers or the excesses of the era of greed he initially flourished in after the Civil War, his target was always human folly and hypocrisy, which turn out to be perennial topics for further study. . . .

The Spanish-American War of 1898 had met with Twain's initial approval because he believed that the U.S. was indeed selflessly bringing freedom to Cuba by helping it throw off the yoke of Spain. But the Eagle had also taken the Philippines as a possession, and by 1899 was waging war against Filipinos who were trying to establish a republic. "Why, we have got into a mess," Twain told the Chicago *Tribune*, "a quagmire from which each fresh step renders the difficulty of extrication immensely greater." The contemporary ring of that assessment is heightened by statistics. By 1902, when Philippine independence had been pretty much squelched, more than 200,000 Filipino civilians had been killed, along with 4,200 Americans.

As Twain got older and was beset by personal tragedies like the death of his beloved daughter Susy, his view of mankind grew darker. He once told his friend William Dean Howells that "the remorseless truth" in his work was generally to be found "between the lines, where the author-cat is raking dust upon it which hides from the disinterested spectator neither it nor its smell." But in 1900, when he could no longer stomach the foreign adventures of the Western powers, he came right out and called a pile of it a pile of it. In the previous year or two, Germany and Britain had seized portions of China, the British had also pursued their increasingly nasty war against the Boers in South Africa, and the U.S. had been suppressing that rebellion in the Philippines. In response, Twain published in the New York *Herald* a brief, bitter "Salutation-Speech from the Nineteenth Century to the Twentieth."

"I bring you the stately matron named Christendom," he wrote, "returning bedraggled, besmirched and dishonored from pirate-raids in Kiao-Chow, Manchuria, South Africa and the Philippines, with her soul full of meanness, her pocket full of boodle, and her mouth full of pious hypocrisies. Give her soap and a towel, but hide the looking-glass." . . .

The new century did nothing to improve his disposition. . . .

Shortly after becoming President, Roosevelt made news by declaring, out of the blue, that "In God We Trust" should be removed from U.S. coins because they "carried the name of God into improper places." Twain responded, in conversation with Carnegie, that "In God We Trust" was a fine motto, "simple, direct, gracefully phrased; it always sounds well—In God We Trust. I don't believe it would sound any better if it were true."

Religiosity prevailed in Twain's era but not in his heart. Though one of his closest friends, Joseph Twichell, was a minister, Twain derided religions—Christianity, in particular—and the notion of a benevolent deity. His strongest written sacrileges were not published, however, until well after his death. He was a more interesting disbeliever in some ways than today's Bill Maher or Sam Harris or Christopher Hitchens, who readily dismiss religion as inflammatory nonsense. Twain, who was full of inflammatory nonsense, could appreciate the indigenous blessednesses he encountered around the world. Stopping in Benares, India, "the sacredest of sacred cities," Twain discovered that "Hindoos" venerate flower-garlanded phallic stones with enormous gusto, which led him to muse on the durability of the impulse to believe. "Inasmuch as the life of religion is in the heart, not the head," he observed, religions are hardy. "Many a time we have gotten all ready for the funeral" of one faith or another, "and found it postponed again, on account of the weather or something."

What put Twain off about religion was its bossiness and its alignment with corrupt community values that people—those standing to profit—insisted on calling a higher power. The very expression "moral sense" made him curl his lip. He denounced his own conscience, which frowned upon his anarchic instincts, his love of enjoyment, and made him feel guilty and rebellious. . . .

As Twain became increasingly angry over the years, less the jester and more the Jeremiah, there was grumbling in some quarters that he had been better when he was funnier. (You could call this the Woody Allen problem.) The New York

Times accused him of "tumbling in among us from the clouds of exile and discarding the grin of the funny man for the sour visage of the austere moralist."

The *Times* had a point. As a social critic, Twain was most enjoyable when he followed his natural humorous tendency to denounce folly and iniquity in all directions. This is what he was doing in *Following the Equator* when he wrote, "All the territorial possessions of all the political establishments in the earth—including America, of course—consist of pilferings from other people's wash. No tribe, however insignificant, and no nation, howsoever mighty, occupies a foot of land that was not stolen. When the English, the French, and the Spaniards reached America, the Indian tribes had been raiding each other's territorial clothes-lines for ages, and every acre of ground in the continent had been stolen and restolen 500 times."

Try rallying a cause with that. . . .

The nation's highest official accolade for comedy is the Kennedy Center's Mark Twain Prize for American Humor, which will be awarded this November to the late George Carlin—another man whose commentary grew bleaker and more biting in his last years. But old Mark, unvarnished, might be too hot for cable, even, today.

Works by Mark Twain

The Celebrated Jumping Frog of Calaveras County and Other Sketches, 1867.

The Innocents Abroad, 1869.

Roughing It, 1872.

The Gilded Age, 1873.

Old Times on the Mississippi, 1875.

The Adventures of Tom Sawyer, 1876.

A Tramp Abroad, 1880.

The Prince and the Pauper, 1881.

Life on the Mississippi, 1883.

Adventures of Huckleberry Finn, 1885.

A Connecticut Yankee in King Arthur's Court, 1889.

The American Claimant, 1892.

Pudd'nhead Wilson, 1894.

Personal Recollections of Joan of Arc, 1896.

Following the Equator, 1897.

The Man that Corrupted Hadleyburg and Other Stories, 1900.

What Is Man? 1906.

Christian Science, 1907.

Extract from Captain Stormfield's Visit to Heaven, 1909.

Mark Twain's Speeches, 1910.

The Mysterious Stranger, 1916.

What Is Man? and Other Essays, 1917.

Annotated Bibliography

Bird, John. *Mark Twain and Metaphor*. Columbia, Missouri, and London: University of Missouri Press, 2007.

In his introduction, the author acknowledges that while both Mark Twain's writing and the concept of metaphor appear to be simple and straightforward, a more layered look at the writer's use of metaphor gives access to much greater depth and complexity than has generally been associated with Mark Twain. Bird suggests that examining Twain's metaphorical language brings the reader into "Twain's "world of hidden desires and dreams, [where we are able to explore] the white fear of the black, the male fear of the female, the despair of the 'damned human race'" (2). This study of Mark Twain's writing assumes some prior familiarity with literary concepts and theories of interpretation.

Budd, Louis J. *Mark Twain: The Contemporary Reviews*. Cambridge: Cambridge University Press, 1999.

This hefty volume contains a chronological listing of each published work by Mark Twain along with a review or reviews that appeared contemporaneously. The editor laments the declining quality of book reviewing employed now more for selling a book than evaluating or understanding it and asserts that much of value can be learned about the culture and worldview of the reading public by reexamining these original responses.

Bush, Harold K. Jr. *Mark Twain and the Spiritual Crisis of His Age*. Tuscaloosa: The University of Alabama Press, 2007.

In his introduction, the author quotes two tellingly different responses Mark Twain had to reading a book about religion and morality: "If I have understood this book aright, it proves two things . . . 1: That Christianity is the very invention of Hell itself; 2 & that Christianity is the most precious and elevating and ennobling boon ever vouchsafed to the world" (1). The first opinion is well known; the second far less so; the author points out that the Ken Burns's PBS documentary, for example, makes almost no reference to Twain's spiritual side. This volume is written to present what the author claims is a more truthfully articulated view of Twain's spiritual and religious engagement.

Clark, Beverly Lyon, ed. *Mark Twain: The Adventures of Tom Sawyer*, A Norton Critical Edition. New York and London: W. W. Norton & Company, 2007.

This volume is explicitly for students. It contains the original full text with footnotes and a brief section on textual variants, comparing the use of words from editions published in 1876, 1980, 1982, and 2007. A section, "Backgrounds and Contexts," offers biographical text, details of nineteenth-century education and medicine, social and regional history, and background on Twain's composition of the work. Another section offers examples of commentary on the novel from its first reviews to recent analyses.

Fishkin, Shelley Fisher, ed. *The Mark Twain Anthology*. New York: Literary Classics of the United States, 2010.

The editor has assembled a large group of diverse voices testifying over the years to the enduring appeal of Mark Twain and his work. She cites in her introduction the views of other major American writers that Twain, above all, represented ideas and qualities of speech that were more quintessentially American than any other writer. Twain, she writes, served, for many, as "guide, goad, and gadfly" (Introduction xv). Twain's sometimes controversial engagement in the politics of his time is given recognition with commentary from European and Asian writers. Lao She, for example, a Chinese writer, expressed appreciation of Twain in 1960 for speaking out about the suffering inflicted by American policy on the Chinese people in California. Writers as diverse as G.K. Chesterton, Helen Keller, Norman Mailer, Dick Gregory, Ralph Ellison, and T.S. Eliot are included.

————, ed. *A Historical Guide to Mark Twain*. Oxford: Oxford University Press, 2002.

This volume—part of an interdisciplinary series on major American writers—distinguishes itself by focusing on the way an author absorbs and then comes to embody and express quintessential aspects of American culture and history. A brief biography is followed by chapters taking up topics, such as race, religion, imperialism, and gender, as they were influenced by and expressed in the author's life. An illustrated chronology and extensive bibliographies make this a valuable study for Mark Twain readers of all backgrounds.

Hutchinson, Stuart, ed. *Mark Twain: Tom Sawyer and Huckleberry Finn*. New York: Columbia University Press, 1999.

This slight book deals succinctly with Mark Twain's best-known novels. After a brief look at Twain's life and work, two chapters follow, one giving the earliest reviews and the second raising some of the contemporary moral questions about *Tom Sawyer*. For *Huckleberry Finn*, a third chapter is added to include the views of this novel by Mark Twain's contemporaries who were also writers.

Kaplan, Fred. *The Singular Mark Twain: A Biography*. New York: Doubleday, 2003.

In the introduction to this biography, the author points out three ways of understanding Mark Twain's "singularity": He "looms" above all other American writers (he is the most frequently quoted and most likely to be regarded as the quintessential American writer); despite being known by two names, he achieved a rare degree of unity; and his name alone evokes images and references to nineteenth-century American cultural and political history. Kaplan moves chronologically through Twain's life, covering an aspect of the author either developed or manifested in a particular time period. For example, the title of chapter 1—"The Best Boy You Ever Had: 1847–1857"—comes from Mark Twain's own reference to himself in a letter he wrote to his mother right after leaving home, hoping to reassure her that he will use the model good judgment other mothers had praised him for having during childhood. Beyond demonstrating his enduring love for his mother, this remark is another example of an apochryphal or made-up Mark Twain story: It was Henry, the youngest, who had actually earned that praise. The volume contains 19 chapters, each written in a way both accessible and entertaining. Three sections of photographs add to this work's appeal.

Lemke, Sieglinde. *The Vernacular Matters of American Literature*. New York: Palgrave Macmillan, St. Martin's Press, 2009.

Citing Ralph Ellison's views about the importance of the vernacular in understanding diverse identities in our culture and linking these ideas with President Barack Obama's views on the importance of working for "a more perfect union," Professor Lemke looks at language use in three discrete ethnic voices—Mark Twain, Zora Neale Hurston, and Ana Castillo—to formulate a new concept of our national literary tradition that emphasizes commonalities.

Loving, Jerome. *Mark Twain: The Adventures of Samuel Clemens*. Berkeley and Los Angeles: University of California Press, 2010.

The author acknowledges in his prologue to this most recent of major studies of Mark Twain (published 100 years after the author's death) not only the sheer number of similar volumes already published but also the likelihood that an entire book has been written on each aspect of Twain's life and work. But, working with the thousands of letters discovered in the last few decades, Loving seeks to retell the Mark Twain story. The book has four parts: Humorist in the West, Writer in the East, The Artist and the Businessman, and The Mysterious Stranger. Each section presents several brief vignettes and observations of which the author writes: "[The] short chapters . . . seek to capture the biological, historical, and to some extent psychological moments of a life that was as long and twisted as the Mississippi River" (7). A brief chronology and many black-and-white photographs are also included.

Messent, Peter, and Louis J. Budd, eds. *A Companion to Mark Twain*. Malden, Mass.; Oxford: Blackwell Publishing, 2005.

This sizeable volume provides a quick but comprehensive guide to Mark Twain's thinking about or relation to dozens of issues and disputes. In part 1, "The Cultural Context," for example, one finds entries about the author and the separate issues of gender, whiteness, and human nature. Part 2, "Mark Twain and Others," discusses the author's relation with William Dean Howells and other southern humorists. Part 3, "Mark Twain: Publishing and Performing," discusses the author's engagement with magazines, the stage, and the screen. Part 4, "Mark Twain and Travel," looks at the author's time in the American West, Europe, and closer to home in Mississippi. Part 5, "Mark Twain's Fiction," looks at individual works including *The Adventures of Tom Sawyer*. Part 6 presents four perspectives on the author's famous humor, and part 7 looks at the evolution and current status of Mark Twain criticism. This volume would be useful for serious students just starting out in Mark Twain studies.

Mitchell, Lee Clark, ed. *Mark Twain: The Adventures of Tom Sawyer*. Oxford University Press, 1993.

This edition of the novel includes a chronology, bibliography, a section of explanatory notes, and commentary by the editor. Mitchell observes the discrepancy between the extravagant attention given to Tom's high jinks and adventures and the paucity of details about any other character. He also laments the absence of a specificity in describing Tom that would give the reader a sense that the character was a real person rooted in a particular time with a personal history.

Morris, Roy, Jr. *Lighting out for the Territory: How Samuel Clemens Headed West and Became Mark Twain*. New York, London: Simon & Schuster, 2010.

The author recalls Huck Finn's fictional sentiments and famous words at the end of *Huckleberry Finn*—"[It's time] to light out for the Territory. . . ."—and likens these to Mark Twain's real journey to the same locations. A map of Twain's stagecoach itinerary starting in 1861 introduces the volume. The author's aim is to show how this "wild west" adventuring generated experiences and insights that contributed to the transformation of Samuel Clemens into Mark Twain.

Quirk, Tom. *Mark Twain and Human Nature*. Columbia, Missouri, and London: The University of Missouri Press, 2007.

This study of Mark Twain focuses on the large belief systems animating and shaping American history in the writer's time. The author sees influences of the Enlightenment, the romantic period in Europe, Calvinism, and Jeffersonian deism. Beginning in 1852, the author looks at groupings of years in Twain's life to understand the confluence of influences with the hope of establishing some idea of how Twain viewed human nature.

Ryan, Ann M. and Joseph B. McCullough, eds. *Cosmopolitan Twain*. Columbia, Missouri and London: University of Missouri Press, 2008.

This recent volume of essays addresses the factor of geographical location as an avenue for reading and understanding who Mark Twain really was and the significance of the way Twain adapted his persona to the different regions of the country he was performing in. The editors assert that this quality of the author has been largely unrecognized, overshadowed by the emphasis on the more accessible persona of the simple, rural, plain-speaking popular storyteller. The contributors to the volume look at the extent of Twain's travels around the United States and abroad, his adaptations and observations of different regions of the world, and his increasingly comfortable ability to appear to be "at home." This quality of cosmopolitanism is the focus of each essay as Twain moves from the most rural regions to the great urban and cultural centers of New York, San Francisco, London, and Vienna.

Scharnhorst, Gary, ed. *Mainly the Truth: Interviews with Mark Twain*. Tuscaloosa: University of Alabama Press, 2009.

According to the editor, Mark Twain was reluctant about giving interviews because his words could be quoted freely from them, and, consequently, he would make less money than he could by "selling" his words himself. He did, however, realize the publicity value interviews carried and so allowed himself to be questioned by journalists and audiences. This collection is organized both by dates and locations. It follows

Twain on his travels around American cities, European countries, and as far away as India, New Zealand, and Australia. Reading the written words of Twain as he spoke them yields a sense of the man not made readily available by his novels. Photographs and illustrations are included.

————, ed. *Critical Essays on "The Adventures of Tom Sawyer."* New York: G. K. Hall & Co., 1993.

The editor of this volume in the Critical Essays series offers a sampling of the earliest reviews of the novel, most of them anonymous, and then turns to more substantive studies made over the past century. He includes voices of praise and appreciation as well as negative commentary.

Sloane, David E. *Student Companion to Mark Twain*. Westport, Connecticut, and London: Greenwood Press, 2001.

As the title suggests, this volume is an accessible introduction to the work and influence of Mark Twain. A section on his life and his contribution to the literature and culture of the United States precedes the separate discussions of individual works. A general bibliography is included as well as briefer listings of critical studies of individual works.

Contributors

Harold Bloom is Sterling Professor of the Humanities at Yale University. Educated at Cornell and Yale universities, he is the author of more than 30 books, including *Shelley's Mythmaking* (1959), *Blake's Apocalypse* (1963), *Yeats* (1970), *The Anxiety of Influence* (1973), *A Map of Misreading* (1975), *Kabbalah and Criticism* (1975), *Agon: Toward a Theory of Revisionism* (1982), *The American Religion* (1992), *The Western Canon* (1994), *Omens of Millennium: The Gnosis of Angels, Dreams, and Resurrection* (1996), *Shakespeare: The Invention of the Human* (1998), *How to Read and Why* (2000), *Genius: A Mosaic of One Hundred Exemplary Creative Minds* (2002), *Hamlet: Poem Unlimited* (2003), *Where Shall Wisdom Be Found?* (2004), *Jesus and Yahweh: The Names Divine* (2005), and *Till I End My Song: A Gathering of Last Poems* (2010). In addition, he is the author of hundreds of articles, reviews, and editorial introductions. In 1999, Professor Bloom received the American Academy of Arts and Letters' Gold Medal for Criticism. He has also received the International Prize of Catalonia, the Alfonso Reyes Prize of Mexico, and the Hans Christian Andersen Bicentennial Prize of Denmark.

Henry Nash Smith (1906–86), a prolific scholar of American writing and culture, is the author of *Virgin Land: The American West as Symbol and Myth* (1950), *Mark Twain: The Development of a Writer* (1962), and *Democracy and the Novel: Popular Resistance to Classic American Writers* (1978). He was responsible for establishing the new academic classification known as American studies.

James M. Cox was a professor of English at Dartmouth College. He is the author of *Mark Twain: The Fate of Humor* (1966); he also wrote about the poetry of Robert Frost.

Judith Fetterley is a distinguished teaching professor of English and women's studies at the State University of New York at

Albany. She co-authored *Regionalism, Women, and American Literary Culture* and authored *Provisions: A Reader from Nineteenth-Century American Women.*

Lee Clark Mitchell has been a professor of English at Princeton. His other published work includes *Witnesses to a Vanishing America: The Nineteenth Century Response* (1981) and *Determined Fictions: American Literary Naturalism* (1989).

E.L. Doctorow is an American writer known for his novels based on nineteenth- and twentieth-century events, including *Welcome to Hard Times* (1960), *The Waterworks* (1994), *Billy Bathgate* (1989), *City of God* (2000), and *The March* (2005). He is a professor of English and American letters at New York University.

Albert E. Stone is professor emeritus of English and American studies at the University of Iowa. He is the editor of *Singula: The Iowa Series in North American Autobiography* and the author of *The Innocent Eye: Childhood in Mark Twain's Imagination* (1961) and *Literary Aftershocks: American Writers, Readers, and the Bomb* (1994).

Michael J. Kiskis is a professor of American literature at Elmira College in New York. He has served as the editor (and co-editor) of *Mark Twain's Own Autobiography: The Chapters of the* North American Review; *Constructing Mark Twain: New Directions in Scholarship*; and *Studies in American Humor.* He is also past president of the Mark Twain Circle of America.

John Bird teaches in the English department at Winthrop University. He edits *The Mark Twain Annual*, a publication of the Mark Twain Circle of America.

Harold K. Bush, Jr., a professor of American literature and culture at Saint Louis University in Missouri, is the author of *American Declarations: Rebellion and Repentance in American Cultural History* (1999).

Roy Blount, Jr., author of 21 books, has also contributed commentary to more than 100 magazines including *The New Yorker* and *The Atlantic Monthly* and served as a journalist interviewing public figures like Ray Charles, Martin Luther King Jr., and Eudora Welty. He is a contestant on the popular National Public Radio show *Wait! Wait! Don't Tell Me.*

Acknowledgments

Henry Nash Smith, "Discovery of River and Town." From *Mark Twain: The Development of a Writer*, Harvard University Press, 1962; reprinted in *Critical Essays on The Adventures of Tom Sawyer*, pp. 79–87, G.K. Hall & Co., 1993. Copyright © 1993 by Gary Scharnhorst.

James M. Cox, "Idyl." From *Mark Twain: The Fate of Humor*, Princeton University Press, 1966; reprinted in *Critical Essays on The Adventures of Tom Sawyer*, pp. 88–102, G.K. Hall & Co., 1993. Copyright © 1993 by Gary Scharnhorst.

Judith Fetterley, "The Sanctioned Rebel." From *Mark Twain: The Adventures of Tom Sawyer: Authoritative Text, Backgrounds, and Contents Criticism*, edited by Beverly Lyon Clark, pp. 279–90. Copyright © 2007 by W.W. Norton & Company.

Lee Clark Mitchell, "Introduction." From *Mark Twain: The Adventures of Tom Sawyer*, edited by Lee Clark Mitchell, pp. vii–xxxiv, Oxford University Press. Copyright © Lee Clark Mitchell 1993.

E.L. Doctorow, "Introduction to *The Adventures of Tom Sawyer*." From *The Mark Twain Anthology*, edited by Shelley Fisher Fishkin, pp. 363–71 Copyright © 2010 by Literary Classics of the United States.

Albert E. Stone, "Afterword. " From *The Adventures of Tom Sawyer*, pp. 1–18. Copyright © 1996 by Oxford University Press.

Michael J. Kiskis, "Mark Twain and the Tradition of Literary Domesticity." From *Constructing Mark Twain: New Directions in Scholarship*, pp. 13–27. Copyright © 2001 by the Curators of the University of Missouri.

Every effort has been made to contact the owners of copyrighted material and secure copyright permission. Articles appearing in this volume generally appear much as they did in their original publication with few or no editorial changes. In some cases, foreign language text has been removed from the original essay. Those interested in locating the original source will find the information cited above.

Index

A

Abu Ghraib photographs, 101
Adult authority, 18
Adult readers, child readers vs.,
  78–81
The Adventures of Huckleberry Finn
  (Twain), 12, 82
Ambivalence, 17, 19
Anderson, Sherwood, 99
Appearance, voice and, 75–78
Audience, ambivalence on, 17, 19
Aunt Polly (character), 21, 24, 27,
  73

B

Background of *The Adventures of
  Tom Sawyer*, 15–20
Bad boy, as hero, 82–83
Baths, 28
Battle scene reenactments, 26–27
Bird, John, 16–17, 91–97
Bliss, Elisha, 19
Blount, Roy Jr., 9, 100–104
Boredom, 44, 70–75
Boy culture, 18
Brooks, Van Wyck, 88, 98
Bugs, 30–32, 72–73
Burns, Ken, 15–16
Bush, Harold K. Jr., 97–100

C

Carlin, George, 104
Carnegie, Andrew, 101
Carroll, Lewis, 81
Casus belli, 26–27
Caves, 55–58
Cecil, L. Moffitt, 32, 33
"The Celebrated Jumping Frog of
  Calaveras County" (Twain), 11,
  12, 91
Characters, overview of, 21–23

Chesterson, G.K., 27
Child readers, adult readers vs.,
  78–81
China, 102
Christianity, Twain and, 28–29,
  103
Church
  boredom and, 71–72
  Bush Jr. on attitudes toward,
    97–100
  funeral scene and, 45–46
  showing off and, 65–67
  Tom's error in, 29–30
  Twain and, 28–29
Civil War, 12
Clairvoyance, 47
Clemens, Clara, 13, 86–87
Clemens, Henry, 13
Clemens, Jean, 13, 86–88, 90
Clemens, John Marshall, 9, 11
Clemens, Langdon, 13
Clemens, Orion, 10, 11, 12
Clemens, Samuel, biographical
  sketch of, 9–14
Clemens, Susy, 13, 87–88
Colbert, Stephen, 9, 100
Commentator, Twain as, 100–104
Commercial values, utopian values
  vs., 42–43
Conflict, introduction of, 62–63
Conformity, 60, 98–99
Conscience, nightmares and,
  36–37, 52
Corruption, money and, 28–29
Cox, James M., 65–70
Crane, Stephen, 83
Cuba, 102
Cure-alls, 37–38

D

Darwinism, 81

"The Death of Jean" (Twain),
86–88, 90
Determinism, 81
DeVoto, Bernard, 62, 82, 88
Dix, Andrew, 42–43
Dobbins, Mister (character),
22–23, 47–48, 50
Doctorow, E.L., 10, 78–81
Douglas, Widow (character), 23

E
Educational reform, 50–51
Eggleston, Edward, 100
Emerson, Ralph Waldo, 15
Epilepsy, 87
Everyman, Tom as, 61
Examination Evening scene,
95–97
Exhibitionism, 45

F
Fearful bewilderment, 54–55
Fetterley, Judith, 30–31, 70–75
Finn, Huck (character), 21, 64
Fly in church incident, 30
Following the Equator (Twain), 104
Freedom, consequences of, 51–52
Funeral scene, 45–46

G
Gerber, John, 16
Gibson, William, on narration, 91
The Gilded Age (Twain), 12, 13

H
Hannibal, Missouri, Twain's
childhood in, 9–10
Harper, Joe (character), overview
of, 21
Harris, Sam, 103
Harte, Bret, 12
Haunted houses, 53, 54
Hemingway, Ernest, 101
Heroes, 61–64, 82–83
Heroin, 38

*History of European Morals from
Augustus to Charlemagne* (Lecky),
28
Hitchens, Christopher, 103
Homesickness, 40, 43
Honorary degrees, 14
The Hoosier Schoolmaster
(Eggleston), 100
Howells, William Dean, 17, 102
Hypocrisy, 15, 24, 27, 71, 73

I
Imperialism, 10–11, 81
"In God We Trust" motto, 103
Individualism, 88
Injun Joe (character)
appearance of, 77
overview of, 23
prejudice against, 23, 56
trapping of in cave, 56
Ink, spilling of, 48
Innocence, 83–84
The Innocents Abroad (Twain), 12

J
Jackson's Island, 42
James, Clive, on democracy, 9
Jones, Welchman (character),
overview of, 23

K
Kaplan, Fred, 11, 14
"King Leopold's Soliloquy"
(Twain), 101
Kiskis, Michael J., 86–91

L
Lampton, Jane, 9
Langdon, Charles, 12–13
Langdon, Olivia Louise, 12–13
Language. *See* Narration;
Vernacular speech
Lawrence, Amy (character),
overview of, 22
Lecky, W.E.H., 28

Lemke, Sieglinde, 15–16
Lewis, Sinclair, 99

M
Maher, Bill, 100, 103
Mark twain (nautical term),
 meaning of, 11
Mark Twain Prize for American
 Humor, 104
Marx, Leo, 42
Mary (character), overview of, 22
Medicines, 37–38
Melodrama, satirizing desire for,
 58–59
Memorization, 28, 29, 99
Messent, Peter, 91
Metaphors, double narrator
 strategy and, 91–94
Misanthropy, 86
Mississippi River adventure,
 39–46
Mitchell, Lee Clark, 45, 54–55,
 75–78
Molson, Francis, 34–35
Money, corrupting influence of,
 28–29
Morris, Linda A., 34–35
Morris, Roy Jr., 9, 12
Motivation, psychology of, 25–26
Narrative intrusions, 25–26
Mufferson, Willie (character), 21
Murder, 34–36, 51–52, 62

N
Narcissism, 45
Narration, 91–97, 99. *See also*
 Vernacular speech
Narrative intrusions, 25–26
Native Americans, prejudice
 against, 56
Nevada Territory, 11, 12
New Deal, origins of term, 14
Nightmares, conscience and,
 36–37, 52
Nobility, 48
Notoriety, 46

O
Ober, K. Patrick, on cure-alls,
 37–38
Objectification, 68
Olbermann, Keith, 100
Opiates, 37–38
Order of the Cadets of
 Temperance, 51

P
Pain-killer cure-all, 37–38
Parody, in chapter XXI, 48–50
Philippines, 101, 102
Pitch bug incident, 30–31, 72
Play, as reality principle, 68–69
Pleasure, commitment to, 68
Points of view, shifting, 16–17
Political commentator, Twain as,
 100–104
Polly. *See* Aunt Polly
Poodle and pitch bug incident,
 30–31, 72
Potter, Muff (character), 23, 51–52
Poverty, 11
Powers, Ron, 98
Prejudice, 10–11, 23, 56, 81
Prudishness, 83
Pseudonyms, 9, 11

R
Racism. *See* Prejudice
Readers, child vs. adult, 78–81
Reality principle, play as, 68–69
Reconstruction, 81
Relationships, inability to navigate,
 88–89
Religion, 28–29, 65–67, 97–100,
 103–104. *See also* Church
Respectability, 60, 63
Riesman, David, 67
Riverboat pilot job, 11–12
Robin Hood, game of, 33, 54
Robinson, Doctor (character), 23
Robinson, Forrest, 11
Rockwell, Norman, 20

Rogers, Ben (character), 21
Roosevelt, Franklin D., 14, 102
Roughing It (Twain), 12

S
"Salutation-Speech from the
Nineteenth Century to the
Twentieth" (Twain), 102
Satire, 9, 98, 100–104
Sawyer, Sid (character), overview
of, 22
Sawyer, Tom (character), 21,
61–64, 70–75
School, 31–32, 72–73
Self-glorification, 45
Sexuality, 83–84
Showing off, 65–70, 98–99
Slavery, 10–11
Smith, Henry Nash, 61–64, 94, 97
Social Gospel, 81
Social injustice, Twain on, 10–11,
100–104
Sound, 34. *See also* Voice
Spanish-American War, 102
Speech, vernacular, 15–16. *See also*
Narration
Sprague, Reverend (character),
overview of, 22
St. Petersburgh, Stone on, 84–85
Stewart, Jon, 9, 100
Stone, Albert E., 81–85
"The Story of the Bad Little Boy
Who Didn't Come to Grief"
(Twain), 18
"The Story of the Good Little Boy
Who Did Not Prosper" (Twain),
18–19, 63

Swimming, politics of, 42–43

T
Telegraph, invention of, 36
Temple, Alfred (character), 21
Thatcher, Becky (character), 22
Thatcher, Judge (character), 22
Theft, 39, 40
Thunderstorm incident, 44
Tick incident, 32, 72–73
Time, arrested, 84–85
Treasure-hunting incident, 53–57
Trilling, Lionel, 15–16
Twain, defined, 11
Twain Prize for American Humor,
104
Twichell, Joseph, 103

U
Utopian values, commercial values
vs., 42–43

V
Values, Kiskis on, 86–91
*The Vernacular Matters of American
Literature* (Lemke), 15–16
Vernacular speech, 15–16. *See also*
Narration
Voice, appearance and, 75–78

W
Walters, Mr. (character), 65–67
Ward, Artemus, 12
Waterboarding, 101
Whitewashing episode, 25 26, 71,
94
Wolff, Cynthia Griffin, 77